THE
LONDON GUIDE,
AND
STRANGER'S SAFEGUARD

AGAINST THE

Cheats, Swindlers, and Pickpockets

THAT ABOUND WITHIN

THE BILLS OF MORTALITY;

FORMING A

PICTURE OF LONDON,

AS REGARDS

ACTIVE LIFE.

BY A GENTLEMAN,
WHO HAS MADE
THE POLICE OF THE METROPOLIS,
AN OBJECT OF ENQUIRY TWENTY-TWO YEARS.

1818.

ANALYTICAL TABLE

OF

CONTENTS.

◆

INTRODUCTION.

WHEN a stranger first arrives in this overgrown city, and finds, upon alighting at the inn, that he has still some miles perhaps to go before he can see his friends, he is naturally anxious for advice how to reach them in safety, with his luggage. But, if this be the case with those who *have* got friends, what is the dread of such as have a home to seek, business to look after, or a place of service to obtain, without a friend to guide their steps, or a candid person to warn them of their danger ; to tell them of the precipices, pit falls, and moral turpitude, of a large proportion of the population of this great metropolis?

To supply the place of a *living friend,* and in some cases to perform the necessary part of one, by directing the stranger in the choice of companions, and what characters he should avoid, I have compiled these sheets ; in which will be found " all 1 know about the matter," and all I could " learn out" by "fine-drawing" of others. In this work I have obtained the assistance of an author by profession, who will new-write it mostly all over. The gentleman will put all of it in order, fit to be read, and add a word or two, or a line or two, here and there, when I am *out*. This is but fair and proper, considering as I am not much used to the pen, I might make "a pretty kettle of fish of it ;" so, "I cares not; not I," says I to the gentleman as employs us both, "its all one to me, though he should strike out every word; for, as for me, as I mean to *out with it all*, he may put it down in what lingo he likes." This is all I shall say " of my own accord," seeing I am willing to make amends for my past life, by disclosing such secrets as never were made public before, not upon paper; and I thought I would have a few words of my own put down in *genuine*, at the beginning, without any of *his* "making or meddling." So, as I have promised and mean to leave off the *calling*, and " live comfortable" upon the profits of this here book, 1 have just put an end to it by *grabbing* three or four books* from the gentleman, my employer, which I have now got under my great coat, as I mean to borrow a word or two, and a few hints as I go on, as is usual in book-making.

Although one of them authors pretends to be up to

---

* 1. Report of the house of commons on the police ; 2. A treatise on the police of the metropolis ; 3. King's Frauds of London ; 4. Sir John Fielding's tracts ; 5. New Monthly Magazine, 1st June, 1817, and Oct. Nov. Dec. and Jan. following.

a great deal, yet he does not know more about the matter than one of us, nor half so much as myself of some things. He had his information from an interested, and therefore a polluted, source,—the officers. When he says, "there are twenty thousand persons of both sexes, who get up in the morning without knowing whereabout they shall sleep at night," he makes a decent good round numbered guess, as applied to one part of the year, but not so as to another, which shows want of discrimination. But what of the fact? Does he propose a remedy? If he had pointed out the means of sheltering them at night, he would have been more beneficially employed; as the statement now stands his readers are left to conclude, "that those twenty thousand houseless wretches are upon the look out for what they can appropriate to themselves." Agreed, as to this inference; and I can tell him, there are an equal number (more) who live in comparative affluence, who are equally upon the alert in *actual robbery*, to say nothing of mere cheats, mace-coves, and such like."

How to steer clear of and to detect these, and a multitude of others, who are always keeping a sharp look out to entrap the property of the honest part of the community, to take in and cheat the unwary,—to rob and perhaps murder the unprotected, and to make a prey of the unsuspecting,—are the motives for this publication. As the information it contains is faithful and genuine, it cannot fail to be highly *useful* to the perambulator and resident Inhabitant, *valuable* as a *guide* to the occasional visitant, and *entertaining* to all descriptions of readers.

As will be seen in the title page, more persons than one have been employed in putting these sheets into their present form; which will account for, and be the apology of a certain discrepancy of style observable in most of the pages; for it was thought better to incur this charge, than to fritter away the pithy sense of the author by grinding it down to the forms and rules of a stubborn rhetoric.

The *terms of art* are explained in the vocabulary; to which the reader may have recourse whenever he is under any difficulty. Among them will be found, also, the English rendering of foreign phrases, which have been retained in the body of the work only because they make part of *the flash* as used by such topping ones as Tom Furby, the young ruffian, Bob Holloway, and such like old ones who knew well how to astonish the natives with scraps of Latin, &c. and who are imitated or copied by great numbers of lads upon every kind of *lay*. Women street walkers of the better sort affect to talk French upon all occasions, as a means of showing their breeding. Tom's Liverpool widow is supposed to have introduced this species of flummery, and no doubt she had it from him.

In avowing the sources whence we have derived our information, we disclaim any intention of 'peaching those we have *fine-drawn*, as well as of having used illegal means of coming at the secrets here disclosed: Were it not for such imputation, we could adduce positive proofs of our accuracy and intimate knowledge of the subjects treated as would convince the most incredulous reader; and as for materials we have such a superabundance as would fill another volume,—intelligence flowing from a hundred quarters, but which is postponed for the present.* Suffice it to say, that some of us have had communications, more or less, with Conkey Beau, Tit Shiels, Bill Soames, Kelting Bight, Hoppy Cole, Mr. Pullen,—little Roberts, Old Smith, Mr. B. Jack Pettit, Bill Colebrook, and almost every living soul mentioned in these pages, at one time or other, or under one garb or another.

N. B. The judicious reader will see, that by our exposing thus accurately the modes of perpetrating crime, those of prevention must become apparent.

In revising these pages as they went to press, we passed over several smaller errors, which fastidious people may say ought to have been amended, from the sentiment that "one may as well be right as wrong." This, however, is not our feeling: we discover our greatest errors to have been these, 1. Spelling a man's name amiss; 2. Attributing the adventure of one man

---

* Shortly will be published, of the same size as this volume, A Companion to the Guide; or the Complete London Tradesman; showing what are the means made use of by honourable men, in conducting their business, trade, or commerce: and also what are the knaveries practised upon upright tradesmen, by the over-keen and disreputable among themselves. By the Editor of " the Guide."

tò another; and 3. Mistaking the strength and quality of some liquor, which we never tasted. If nothing more important than these occur, we shall congratulate ourselves upon having attained a degree of perfection we by no means hoped for in the earlier stages of our labours : should such have crept in, however, we beg the favour of candid readers to point them out upon paper, directed to W. Perry, left at No. 6, Holborn Barrs.

May, 4th, 1818.

Erratum : Page 115, line 6, for *dark* read *dank*.

Reader, a pocket book.
Roost, bed.

Sanctum Sanctorum, Latin, inner or sacred place.
Scamps, ragged street thieves.
Seedy, shabby dress. No money.
Slang, covert language of thieves.
Snuffy, drunkish.
Snoozing Ken, a sleeping house.
Spar, fighting demonstrated.
Spree, fun.
Spill (*to*) to betray.
Stag (*to*) to look hard at; as stags or deers do on all intruders.
Sweet, kind, concilating.

Take In, a cheat.
Take it In, to swallow a lie.
Thing, (a) a robbery.
The Things, stolen articles.
Toggery, clothing.
Touting, eyeing the women, generally.
Town, London.
Upon the Town, street walkers, men or women.
Trade, (the) smuggling.
Transmogrify, to change.
Turned Up, ruined.
To have *Turnips* (turn-ups) a refusal or denial.
Twig (to) to eye one particularly.

Vestal, ironical for an incontinent person.
Verburn Sat Latin, means—" a word to the wise is enough,"

Whop, a blow or slap.

THE
LONDON GUIDE,

&c. &c. &c.

◆

INN YARDS AND COACHES.

Most people come up to town by coaches and waggons, a few on foot, and fewer still by water; therefore the inns at which the former put up, are places of especial resort for thieves and cheats of a better sort. The little public houses on the outskirts, as well as those along shore, are frequented by a very ordinary and more desperate set. All are upon the sharp look-out for dupes; the innocent, the artless, and the unwary, are alike their prey. The very sight of a countryman sharpens their appetite, especially if he brings his wife with him, because she embarrasses his movements. I cannot then compare

B

the expression of their countenances to any thing
so like, as that of a sportsman when he sees a
covey of partridges rise from the stubble.—
Sometimes the likeness is greater, when two sharpers, like two sportsmen, pursuing the same game,
meet unexpectedly : "What are you after?"
demands one. "Catching of flats," is the reply;
and they cordially join in hunting down their
prey.

Smashing is the first depredation to which
strangers are exposed, upon setting foot in London, and consists in passing bad money in change,
or pretending you yourself have paid such base
coin. Without particularising any one description of characters at the inns, who would be more
likely than another to practise this species of
cheatery, I must be allowed to say, they are all
liable—Coachmen, guards, clerks, and waiters—
to be themselves imposed upon, and although
not *guilty*, are nevertheless likely to pass bad
money. The original evil arises with fellows who
hang about the inn yards, pretending to make
themselves *useful*, or selling and buying some
article or other ; some of these we shall have occasion to say a word or two about, under the
title of " JOBBERS," and others called " DUF-
FORS or BUFFORS."

Thus, while we are yet writing, it is placed upon record, that the *hangers-on*, or helpers, at the great public inns, are engaged in the most dangerous species of cheatery; one of those *useful* persons, at the Swan with Two Necks, Lad-lane, was brought to Hatton Garden office, January 28, 1818, charged with passing bad notes, &c. " He had been in the habit, for *four years* before, of procuring customers to go by their coaches, for which he received a pecuniary reward," said the clerk at that inn : to this information Mr. John Lees, inspector of bank notes at the Bank of England, stated to the magistrates, " that there was scarcely a coach-office in town but forged notes (similar to that now produced from the *Swan)* had been passed at, and after-wards brought into the bank."

About a year before this, a " jobber," one George Meacock, who " *hung-about*" the Queen's Head, corner of St. John's Street, for years, under the appearance of a general dealer and smuggler, and was supposed to be rich, since he lived com-fortably,—was hanged for the same offence. He was always furnished with good *smooth whites ;* which, according to *the time of day,* was the *flash* for bad shillings, as *screens* is for forged notes of the Bank of England.

The name of the first-mentioned culprit is James Law, quite a youth, who will, probably, receive the reward of his early crimes about the time of the appearance of this publication. How can the honester part of those who are engaged about inn yards avoid coming in contact, and partaking in the corruption, while they are daily in the habit of seeing so many others actively employed in such nefarious transactions, as the passing bad money, or the representations of money? To what extent it is carried, with such means at their disposal, remains to be guessed at, since there is no probability of making a calculation. As bad silver is always stirring in great abundance at the inns, so upon the road; those of the drivers who have been contaminated, seldom give change without tendering base money, more or less: it happens at times that they give *nothing but bad*, so that the cheat is not discoverable upon comparison.

Not only must the New comer be upon his guard against bad-money, but must be as much prepared to meet the less refined depredator who would purloin his boxes and other baggage.

As soon as a coach enters an inn yard, it is followed or met by persons, who either *actually* expect friends by it, or *pretend* they do; to-

gether with those idle fellows who constantly
hang about coach yards, without other visible
means of livelihood than what they can pick up,
and are therefore said to be " upon the *kedge.*"
But inn yards are nothing like so much infested
as they were twenty years ago, because of the
officers, who take away the offenders, " when
they are wanted," but not until then, as it
would not be worth their while. A complete
clearance might be made, but the men not having
done any thing *capital,* that is to say, *rewardable by statute,* the officers do not choose to interrupt them, and they accordingly go on nibbling, until something great turns up,—and then
justice interferes.

The plan is, when *the things* lie about promiscuously, for the thief to become officious, as
if willing to be serviceable; he looks about in a
simple manner, asks an unmeaning question of
one or other of the passengers, as if they were
well known to each other; and then turning
about with a smile, he takes up some box or
bundle which he pretends to carry towards the
house, or to the scales (as the case may be) where
the baggage *ought* to go, still keeping near to, or
talking with the same passenger as before. Meanwhile, having taken a view of all being clear out

of sight, he bolts off in quick time; next takes to his heels, and making a double turn or two round the corners, he eludes pursuit, much less detection.

Coachmen and guards, belonging to the mails and stage coaches, are mostly honest men, as the times go; many of them are of high character, and some become proprietors, and defy the world. But the practices of "shouldering" passengers, on their own account—doing *the natives* out of articles of life, which they bring to town to dispose of—the dealing in contraband goods, and a number of other out-of-the-way methods,—to say nothing of the wish to appear over-cunning,— bring them to " take care of things," for which there is no immediate owner. The feelings once blunted by one improper pursuit, leave their owner open to the fascinations of another, till at length the *quality* of the crime is no longer an object of solicitude.

This remark is more pointedly applicable to *short* stage and hackney coachmen; the latter of whom are mostly " turned-off characters"—a few are " returned lags;" of course neither the one or the other are to be trusted out of sight,— nor yet scarcely in your sight.

If gloves, a handkerchief, a shawl, or other

small article be left in the coach, it may be known by Jarvy's taking off his hat and placing it in the coach; then holding the door tight behind him, he deposits the article *found* in the poll of his hat, which he puts on his head.

N. B. Whatever coachman manœuvres the door of his coach, he is at no good : the hackneyman keeps *his* open to prevent his *number* from obtruding itself upon your notice ; the stagecoachman keeps his tight against his back, the better to conceal what he is at. The landlord of the tap, or watering house, the next barber's shop, or cobbler's stall, are the places to enquire what is become of *the things*, generally speaking.

At every inn yard there are a kind of " hangers on," as we mentioned higher up, who are men of the worst character, since they affect an integrity they do not possess, and therefore are sometimes entrusted when they ought not to be. They are vastly familiar with the people really employed ; they run of errands, and carry messages; and if there is a *thing to be done* upon the sly, they get off with impunity, because the person whose immediate business it should be to detect him, is induced to wink at, in hopes of sharing the depredation. Sometimes they hang about the tap-room for entire days, to hand off what may come to hand (by the coaches) either of contraband or of stolen property; at other times they are employed to stand at some given place— as the corner of an avenue, or under the gateway, to catch hold of what may be thrown down to them from the coaches, with a view either to cheat the proprietors, the revenue, or the right owners. See more on this subject under the head of "wagering kiddies," or gamblers of the lower sort.

Most guards have a particular *tune* upon their horns for every different species of service, known only to each his own particular dependant, which gives a wonderful facility to their manœuvres. I have sat down with the landlord of a tap-room, who, without looking out, would remark, "here comes such-a-one;" "Jemmy is in first," and the like notice, showing his great familiarity with the tunes : and then again "run out and pick up ——'s basket;" or "here's a pig coming this time." In this manner giving facility to the concealment and disposal of ill-gotten articles of life.

In the year 1815, the G——— mail brought up one hundred and twenty pieces of India handkerchiefs weekly—forty in a bundle. No one could imagine how such an article should come

from that place; nor is it our business or inclination to enquire how they got there. It was pleasant to see the hangers-on scamper away with the
square bundle of a morning; sometimes from
one point, sometimes from another, taking care
not to make their deposit at the same place too
often.

From all this, the reader must be aware, that
persons so employed, are not trustworthy with his
luggage, and that he would do well to see after
it with his own eyes; for if he permit one of the
officious hangers-on to meddle with it, no opportunity will slip by unimproved, even though
the coachman and guard are standing near. These
are not a check sufficiently strong upon his dis-
honesty, since he is himself *down* to so many of
their tricks—such as "shouldering," and the
like, that they dare not interfere in his "nibbling."

Shouldering, among coachmen, is that species
of cheating in which they take the fares and
pocket them, generally of such passengers as they
overtake on the road, or who come across the
country; but it not unfrequently happens that
they take passengers the whole line of their run,
even when the proprietors scarcely have one inside for themselves. A curious story of this na-

ture is told by an old man in Lad Lane, that
when he and a certain *great man* there, were upon the same coach, not one of six inside passengers were down upon the way-bill; and, that he
having proposed to give their employers at least
one of them, the *great man* threatened to kick
him for this puling conduct, and did actually
collar him; and applied to him the words—
" fool, rascal, and b —— thief." Thus it is,
the worst spoke in the wheel generally cries out
the first.—*They " shouldered" the whole six !*

Those who travel much by stage coaches,
should always take care to see themselves booked,
as in case of accident, they cannot recover damages against the proprietors without it.

Every one knows (and their employers know it)
that hackney coachmen invariably share with
their masters in large proportions. Those often
get good prizes left in their coaches, by people
who carelessly leave their boxes or parcels behind, in the hurry to meet their friends ; or what
is more general, those who take out their papers,
money, pocket-book, &c. to look over in a
hackney coach, in order, as they think, to save
time, too often leave some part behind them ; or,
by the motion of the coach get it jostled out of
their hands. At no time has a hackneyman been

known to restore to its rightful owner such things
as may have been so left, at the earliest opportunity, nor unless a *handsome* reward is offered.

By the way, the number of a hackney coach
should be always noted the moment it is *called*
(or ordered) ; and in so " calling" them, as well
as every word that is said to the coachman, a
certain air of command or authority should be
kept up. This holds them to their tethers; tells
them they have no green-horn to deal with, and
deters them from extorting too much for the fare.
If a person, meekly or hesitatingly, gives his orders, the coachman and attendant *waterman* pass
the word " Johnny Raw ;" or if it be a lady,
they protract the sound of " Ma'am" to her ;—
thus, " yes M-a-a-m" and " no M-a-a-a-m."

When a coach is called from the stand, the
waterman opens the door as it draws near you, in
order to prevent the number, which hangs on it,
from obtruding itself on your sight : at setting
down, the coachman, with the same view, keeps
open the door whilst he gets paid, especially if
there be a dispute; or, if he *twigs* something
left behind, he slaps the steps or the door, so as
to make the horses move on a step or two; he
then halloos at them with who-o-o; swears a good
peal of oaths at them, to intimidate his cus-

tomers, and then resumes the dispute, if convenient.

If a hackney coachman be a smasher, or dealer
in bad silver, he endeavours to set down his fares
(by night) in a dark place, if possible, in total
disregard of your orders, generally quarrels with
his horses, should be be obliged to take them by
the heads,—which quarrel is sometimes meant
for his customers. He most frequently " throws
off," or talks to his horses of " the precious good
looking load they have been " dragging :" " no
great shakes; I'll bet a pound of my *own money*,"
he will say, while making the animals stand ;
and if you supervent his attempts at smashing,
he mounts his box, with the observation—" You
knows about as much as *I* do, *mastee* ;" but if
you reply sharply, rebuking his impertinence, he
does not hesitate to charge you with crime, by
inuendo, as " Vhere did you come from? I
vonder !" making a motion as if you had come
from a prison; and adding, " you'll soon be
bowled out, I'll be bound." Such is a fair
sample of the conduct of the far greater number
of hackney coachmen.

SMASHING is managed thus—a bad shilling or
two, or a half-crown, is placed in the left hand
between the fingers, and the hand is then half-

closed upon them; which operation is performed while he tugs at the coach door to let you out. —(Those who smash under other circumstances have more leisure to prepare themselves). Should " the fare" want change for a pound note, the result is no longer doubtful : three or four shillings, *at least*, " come to his share." But the chiefest ingenuity is, to persuade you that you yourself have tendered bad money to poor Jarvis ; who, after turning your money over and over, and perhaps taking a trial upon the stones, declares they *ring bad*, and you must change them for good ones. If you appear tolerably " *soft*," and will " stand it," he perhaps refuses these also, after having " rung the *changes*" once more. This is called " a double do;" and then, lest the transaction may have been " stagged" by some impertinent by-stander, or *a trap*, he mounts his box, and drives away with the utmost precipitancy.

N. B. Whenever a hackney coachman thus drives off in a great hurry, rely upon it 'something is the matter ; in which case, he does not pull up at the *next* coach stand, but drives past it, '" standing for no repairs."

Every one should be apprized, the moment they arrive in town, or rather before they enter it, of the absolute necessity there is of taking the number of a hackney coach as soon as it is called. Servants ought to have this salutary precaution impressed on their minds; as also, that as soon as any company comes to the door of their masters in a hackney coach, they should set down in their memories, if not in chalk or in ink, what number it bears. If a reward were paid for such vigilance, when any thing has been recovered by that means, it would add to the stimulus, and have an increasing good effect.

WALKING THE STREETS,

As well as riding is effected more securely by affecting an ease or knowingness, which deters imposition in a great degree. We spoke higher up of assuming an air of authority in giving orders to hackney coachmen; no less serviceable is it to *appear* like a thorough bred cockney in your gait and manner, by placing the hat a little awry, and with an unconcerned stare, penetrating the wil· countenances of the rogues, you attain one more chance, at least, of escaping the snares that are always laid to entrap the countryman or new comer: these latter are easily recognised by their provincial gait, dialect, and cut of the cloth; by the interest they take in the commonest occurrences imaginable, and the broad stare of

wonder at every thing they see. Such men attract
the attention of passers-by of *every* degree; and,
it would be surprising indeed, if the knavish part
of the community did not endeavour to profit by
the want of knowledge apparent in Johnny New-
come, or Johnny *Raw*, as such men are aptly
called. He is followed for miles, sometimes for
an entire day or more, by a string of pickpockets
or highwaymen, until they can find an opportunity to *do* him. It came out on the examination
of Sethard, for robbing A. Anderson, that he
and his companions had followed their victim from
the waterside to Mincing Lane, thence to *the
Hercules*, in Leadenhall Street, where the foolish
man counted over his money; thence to Snow
Hill, and back again to the corner of St. Martin's
le-Grand, where they hustled and robbed him of
near seventy pounds, the hard earnings of twenty
years at sea; and all this by broad day-light!

Walking the streets has been reduced to a
system in London; every one taking the right
hand of another, whereby confusion is avoided;
thus, if you walk from St. Paul's towards the
Royal Exchange, you will be entitled to the wall
of those you *meet* all the way; whereas, if you
cross over, you must walk upon the kirb stone.
The contrary mode is a sure indication of a person

being a stranger, or living at the outskirts of
town, and is certain of attracting attention to his
awkwardness (a thing always to be avoided.)   A
pickpocket will hustle such an one against his
accomplice in the day time; the stranger will be
irritated no doubt, and express his indignation,
which will be the better for the rogues : in a
half-minute's altercation, they get the best of
the jaw, because the loudest and most impudent;
—a *spar* or two ensues, in which he who pretends
to support the stranger to the ways of town, draws
him of his pocket-book, or his watch, if he has
either, a fact they take care to ascertain before-
hand.   *Money* in the *breeches* pockets, can only
be come at in a crowd, or by *flooring* the victim;
the former of which is most usually, but the latter
very seldom, performed in the day-time.

From all this, my reader will see the necessity
of cautiously, yet energetically, pursuing his
way, without dread or doubt ; since it is better
to walk a little out of the right path, than run the
risk of being *directed* wrong : to steer clear of
assemblages in the streets, by going round them,
or pressing rather rudely through them ; whereby
you become the *assailant*, if I may be allowed
the term, and add one more chance of steering
clear of danger.

PICKING OF POCKETS.

This way of obtaining the property of others, is certainly the most genteel, profitable, and alluring of any, because it requires some degree of ingenuity to exercise it properly, and a great deal of address and firmness to get off without detection. Professors of the art are admired for their dexterity, by every one but the immediate losers; and people laugh at the droll way in which the sufferers relate how they were *done*. I have myself seen two friends just as they found out that one of them had lost his Reader or Tattler; —to see the vacant stare of the one, and the broad grin of the other, was to me as high fun, almost, as the actual possession of the property. Even magistracy itself seldom looks half so glum upon a predatory marauder of this order as he does upon a night robber, a housebreaker, or a highwayman. Whenever the prosecution is brought up to the point of conviction, the prosecutor always leans to the side of mercy; and the *capital* is " taken off:" one never hears of a pickpocket being hung.

Lagging is the worst they can come to. Lucky dog that I was, in adopting so safe, so genteel, and such a productive part of the calling ! Whatever may be said of it, now I have given over the pursuit, I must say I have done a violence to my taste, as an amusement, however good the relinquishment may be as to morals.   If the opportunity were to arrive of choosing again, I scarcely know which line of conduct I should take; but having so taken it, I am determined to be sincere, and I mean to be a little more particular in the details of this my favourite pursuit than upon other topics ; although these are all collected out of the mouths of each the first in his profession, living or dead, at home and *abroad*.

Although the officers constantly patrole the streets, or ought to do so, yet they suffer well-known thieves to mix in the crowds that assemble around print-shops, and other showy exhibitions of goods.   If a horse tumbles, or a woman faints, away they run to encrease the crowd, and the confusion ; they create a bustle, and try over the pockets of unsuspecting persons ; till at length, having marked out one, the accomplice shoves him hard up against other persons, (perhaps some of the gang) who naturally repress the intrusion.   Thus wedged in, they next hit him on the head (more or less hard), when he, to save his hat, or to resent the insult, lifts up his arms, a

third or a fourth still farther behind gives one
more shove, rams his flat hand against the belly
of the person marked out to be *done*, and pulls
out his watch. .. If it be his pocket-book they are
after, they lift up the skirts of his coat to come at
his inside pocket; but should it lie on his breast,
then the rogue, who is next to the victim, seizes
his collar and drags until the buttons give way,
or there is space enough between the coat and
the body for the accomplice to thrust in his arm.

So situated, it is clear that every other pocket
must be liable to a visit, the breeches not except-
ed. As he in the rear is generally a *short* man,
or a boy, he thrusts in underneath the arms of
the accomplices, who make room for him on purpose, and he is thus enabled to pick two or three
pockets at leisure, especially in large crowds;
such as a boxing match, or my Lord Mayor's
Show. Upon the last mentioned occasion, the
chief place for the sport is Ludgate Hill, though
the whole range from Blackfriars to Guildhall
affords a fine harvest, from the moment *my lord*
takes water to his return home. On that day
the gangs assemble regularly, and enter the city
at various points. For many years the practice
has been to station two women, of good stout
growth, near the place of operation, who receive

the few stray articles that may be picked up before the grand rush is made, when they join in,
and increase, the confusion. Some ten or twelve
men, mostly armed with sticks, are attached to
these women, and act in concert on one side of
the hill, while a gang similarly composed take
the other side, and numerous smaller detachments,
and single rogues, are strewed about in all
directions.

As the procession advances, the first object is
to create a bustle, and if possible a fight. They,
therefore, inclose between them a few people of
respectable appearance, and press them forward
rudely ; those in front resent this, pretending to
be offended, and thrust back those next to them ;
the sticks go to work upon the heads, and the accomplice embracing his fellow, reaches round at
the fob, or pockets of the victim, whose hands are
employed in protecting his head.

The trunk-maker's corner was, for many years,
the spot for making a stand at ; and the articles
stolen used to walk up the Old Bailey to Whet-
stone-park corner. But things of this sort must
change in a course of years, for the very circumstance of this exposure must of necessity compel
alteration, to prevent detection. Yet again, on
consideration, this is not so certain, since there

are not a greater set of fools in the world that
your hackneyed thieves : they have been known
to throw themselves in the way of certain detection, or, to stand, like the silly penguin, to be
knocked down ; when, at the same time, a good
run for it, would have preserved them in safety.

N. B. But should a pickpocket take to his heels,
and be easily distinguished from his followers, it
is not always advisable to stop him ; unless indeed, you are fond of a bit of a *spree*, or admire
being in trouble, as is exemplified in the simple
narrative of a writer " on the police," who has not
thought proper to give us his name.   He says,
" that he detected a daring noon-day robber, and
brought him to conviction.*" Again, he observes,
" To be candid, I must confess that my cure for
stagging, was accelerated by means of certain
bruises and fractures which I received from the
hands of three or four of these gentry, and that
close to my own house. Very few shopkeepers
would undergo a *second time*, so much trouble
and expence as I then did; and, therefore, I do not
blush to avow that I forfeited my recognizance
in one instance, and have passed over the detection of several others to avoid consequences so

---

* See New Monthly Magazine, 1st June, 1817—signed
" A Constant Reader." page 309.

inimical to my repose." What is more, they can
mostly fight a bit, and some are armed with
knives, which they would not hesitate to use in a
scuffle.

Strangers, and silly persons, who are the chief
objects with the pickpockets, are not better
known by their first appearance, than from the
ill-advised custom of *asking the way*, and standing gaping at the names of the streets, as if in
doubt which road to take. This being a sure
indication that they are at a loss, and of course
confused, such a person is perhaps accosted, and
misdirected into some street or lane more adapted
to the robbers' purpose; and there met again, or
overtaken by one, two, or three others, he is
either *hustled*, or his *pockets neatly picked*, or he
is *knocked down* with a bludgeon. Therefore it is
recommendable, that no one should ask his way
in the streets, but in decent shops, or, at most,
of persons carrying small parcels, which indicate
they are shopmen or porters : thieves do not go
about encumbered in that manner, at least not
hitherto ; but they might possibly adopt it hereafter, from this hint, as the best method of
catching flats. Never ask your road of a gentleman, in appearance ; if he be a real one, he either
will not condescend to answer, or more probably

does not know any more than yourself ; and for
a better reason—that thieves frequently go well-
dressed, especially pickpockets ; good *toggery,*
being considered a necessary qualification for his
calling, without which the *Diver* could not possibly mix in genteel company, nor approach such
in the streets.   But the close observer may always discover in the dress of the genteel pickpocket, some want of unity, or shabby article, as
a rusty hat, or the boot-tops in bad order, or a
dirty shirt and cravat: He may come at the
same conclusion, by noticing an article of dress
which has been made at the top of the mode,
some long while before the other parts of his
dress, together with similar attempts to appear
the would-be gentleman of *ton.*   Mr. Pullen
was, however, an exception to this general rule :
the neatness and uniformity of his rigging, from
top to toe, his cleanliness, the mild smirk of his
red face, and at length his age, contributed to
render him as truly respectable looking a pickpocket, as we shall ever find again. A curious
proof how far this feeling regarding Mr. Pullen
may be carried, will be learnt from the following
anecdote. Mr. Pullen found occasion to go into
a public house at some part of town distant from
the usual haunts. He was here in close conver-

sation with two gentlemen, when the master of
the house beckoned him out, and gave him *leave
of absense.* " I shall go instantly,—but my cane
and gloves lie in that corner," replied Mr. Pullen. To this Boniface objected, ordered him to
" evacuate the premises," without *the goods,* and
proceeded to acts of violence ; the two strangers
interfered, protected " the respectable looking
old gentleman," as they called him, disbeliev-
ing the landlord's information, which they attri-
buted either to a hoax, or to malice, and went off
in triumph to another house. What is more,
they handed him along arm in arm between them,
and he could scarcely get liberty to speak a word
to a nice crummy young woman, who seemed
surprised and interested at his situation. " He
wished to send home a message by her," he said ;
but the two boobies would not lose sight, and
did but just loosen their hold. The interview
was abridged by their intrusion, and with the use
of a little force, the fair frail one was permitted
to pursue her way.

But what a tragedy ! One of the strangers lost
his pocket-book, soon after he had occupied his
present seat, as he said, and the other a small
packet of less value. They suspected their new
acquaintance, and he was searched by consent,

but nothing was found upon him, though the packet was discovered under a chair at a distant part of the room. As none of the parties had gone out ; they were the more puzzled the more they thought how it could have been lost. The fact is, briefly, that the female carried it off; the loser having been mistaken in saying, he had felt it since he entered the room ;—a warning to people how cautious they should be in stating unnecessary particulars, too hastily.

Here was a very *neat* and *clean* job done, and all safe and right ; and is that sort of practice which for distinction's sake is termed " picking of pockets," simply ; though hustling, and knocking down, or tripping up are the same thing prastised, with more violence. We will, therefore, describe all those methods as carried on against single persons.

The pickpocket who does the thing " neatly," as the phrase is, goes alone ; or, at most, two together. His intention is not to use violence, and he even avoids being *felt* at work ; for which reason the law has made it *capital* felony to execute his task so adroitly as not to be discovered *in the act of taking*; notwithstanding which law, he always endeavours to incur the highest crime,

while the judge as invariably apportions to him,
the lesser punishment.

For the accomplishment of his purpose, he
walks the crowded streets, and tries the pockets
of various passers by ; till at length he finds the
situation of the *pocket-book*,—which has been the
favourite aim ever since the extensive circulation
of bank-notes. If it occupies the outer coat
pocket, the task is easy : he dips his hand into
the pocket, spreading his fingers to keep open
the top, and with the forefinger and thumb draws
it forth. Sometimes out it comes, easily, which
will be the case if not near so large as the pocket;
but should it stick, or hang by something else,
the rogue *stands no repairs*, but pulls away by
main force.

During the first part of the operation, and previously, he has walked a step or two cheek-by-
jowl with the person to be robbed ; he looks
about smiling, (to take off the attention of those
who may be near behind,) as if they were acquaintance, and the thing a mere matter of
course and familiarity. A thin worn-out great
coat, flowing open, is an excellent screen.

If the thing to be *drawn* is heavy, and its
weight might be instantly missed, he presses
equally hard upon the edge of the pocket, or

stoops a little to take hold of the bottom, gives a jirk, steps upon the heel, or jostles against the person *done ;* then seems to beg pardon, and runs. For the inside skirt coat-pocket, he lifts up the skirt or tail, and out comes the pocket-book. Should a button impede the way out, a little knife, fastened to the hand, soon removes that obstacle.

N. B. Whenever you are jostled against, or your heel is trodden upon, you may suspect that person, and he who is nearest to you on the other side.

Two are much safer to get off than one, as the second keeps a good look-out; and he it is that goes off with the prize, having received it from him who first took it. This one, being next to the victim, if seized, as is most likely, kicks up a row, and uses the most disgusting language; or, in quite other tones, offers to pursue him who has gone off; but in fact, in pursuing, throws obstacles in the way of others; but should he come up with, and overtake him in the hand of justice, they together fight away if possible to effect an escape; sometimes dropping the thing stolen, at other times it gets handed to a confederate, who perhaps has the audacity to claim the property as his own.

Many women are as expert as men, and they always have one or two at hand upon great occasions, as I said before. They are furnished with a species of pocket which completely encircles their bodies, coming down half way to the knees; if the wearer be somewhat stout and bulky, it is clear she can conceal a good deal. Besides, if she be searched upon suspicion, the articles will traverse from before to behind, and back again, with a very small quantity of dextrousness; and she would thus elude discovery by any *ordinary* scrutiny of her person. The same sort of pocket is used in shop-lifting.

Women who walk the streets at night, are invariably pickpockets; and I see no reason to set down those who by day entice the men into their dens, any thing better. Such as stand at the corners of lanes and courts, inviting men to stop, are clumsy hands, but contrive to pick up a good harvest occasionally: they rob indiscriminately every article of dress, knocking off the silly (perhaps drunken) man's hat in the street, with which the accomplice runs away; at other times they will take off his cravat, while bestowing upon him their salacious caresses. A broach, or shirt-pin, is constantly made good prize of, but should the deluded man enter one of those pestiferous abodes, which are so numerous in this metropolis, the loss of all he has is inevitable.

N. B. It is recommended over again not to be stopped in the streets, even by a *handsome* woman, though that should be by day. They have great nimbleness of fingers, and convey away your property while talking you into a silly passion for their persons,

Although it seems brutish to rebuke a woman who should press against you in a crowd, in a church, at an auction, or in the streets, yet this should be done. At the Rev. Rowland Hill's meeting house, the women attend as well as the men pickpockets; they are found amongst the crowd of a procession to St. Paul's, and in fact at every collection of people. Such women amuse you with asking silly questions; perhaps complain to you of some man who is pressing her, while one of her accomplices rifles your pockets in the mean time, from behind another accomplice, who keeps his arms up so as to prevent yours from defending your property. Perhaps she seizes your arm, as if for protection, but in fact to keep you from using it.

One very excellent trick for a woman to perform is, to turn round quick upon the gentleman to be robbed, and running hard against him,

endeavour to touch him in the wind, pretending
herself to be very much hurt.   Her accomplices
are behind, and improve upon the *accident*, by
embracing the victim ; and the hindermost is
generally the thief who hands off the property.
It must be present, to every one's mind, that
when a person is hit upon the belly, or pit of the
stomach—and those women are taught how to
place their blows—he will naturally bend from
the effects of the blow : At that moment it is,
he loses his watch, a *dive* is made into his breeches
pocket, and both are drawn ; and if the lady's
hurt is very bad, (that is, well played off) his
pocket-book goes to wreck also.

This same trick of turning round, is also
practised by two or three men ; and a good
method is to stoop suddenly down, whereby the
person to be robbed comes wholly, or in part, to
the ground ; and during the struggle to recover
himself, or the efforts of the accomplice to assist
him, the job is effected.

Ladies who press to the windows of drapers
shops are fine game.   When they wore pockets
with hoops, scarcely any operation in all the light
finger trade was easier than the *dive*, or putting
in one's hand ; afterwards, on the disuse of the
hoop, the thing was performed by a short fellow,

or boy, getting between the legs of the accomplice (a tall one) and spreading the petticoats, cut off the pockets, with a knife attached to the hand.

The practice of *cutting* pockets is much lessened of late years, why, I know not for certain; but apprehend the fear of incurring the penalty of Lord Ellenborough's act, may have had its effect; and since there are several methods of achieving the same thing, there could be no possible reason why the safest should not be adopted. Any other course of proceeding would be foolish, to say no worse of it. A capital small blade, set in a ring for the middle finger, or the thumb, was a much better contrivance than the common penknife, or the sliding blade; because their right hand can be employed in cutting, and *grabbing* the money at one and the same time, whilst the left is engaged no less usefully in bothering his *gob*. This latter, is nothing more than placing the flat hand (back or palm) over the mouth, (or *gob*) of a fellow who is likely to, *sing out;* at the same time taking care that it shall seem to him the effect of accident, not capable of being reckoned uncivil, if the business should come to a *patter*. In all mobs where there is not sufficient noise, this bothering the *gob*, is invariably had recourse to; the fellow might otherwise call out "pickpockets," or some such stuff, when he felt the things going from his person. ·

Notwithstanding the generally received notion, that pickpockets are an innocent race of mortals, who merely purloin a little of your pelf, yet nothing can be more contrary to the real fact.   No means of escape would be left untried, in case of detection, even although that should cost the life of an individual or two.   They are invariably taught boxing, *scientifically*, women as well as men ; I mean, so far, as how to place a blow or two with the *happiest* effect. Indeed, picking of pockets frequently assumes the character of footpad robbery, having all its characteristic features of force, and violence of conduct on the part of the perpetrators.   This brings me to speak of that next species of robbery by those who are appropriately termed *Scamps,* called

HUSTLING ;

Which is performed in various ways, as suits the present situation of both parties. Higher up, I described the way in which the persons to be *done,* are crammed together, in order to be robbed.   The next degree of violence is that where the arms are seized from behind by one, whilst the other *frisks* the pockets of their contents.

Just the same end is obtained by picking an instant quarrel, and collaring the victim, pull him forward ; while he is thus upon the stoop, the accomplice takes a *dive* into his pockets, handing off whatever he may find to a third accomplice, who perhaps has been making free use of his stick promiscuously over the heads of all parties. Another plan is to seize him by the collar of the coat behind, and pull him backwards: he must be a rum customer, indeed, if he gets over this, and a dig in the guts in front ; for having lost wind, he will not recover it again until his property is irrecoverable.

A more daring hustle is, where a person being run against violently, as if by accident, and his arms kept down, forcibly ; while the accomplice, pretending to take " the gentleman's" part; draws either his watch, money or hook. More cannot well be done in an instant thing like this. Should the pair come down *whop*, it is far the better for the thieves ; they both get up, pardon is begged, and they part as quickly as possible. The sufferer, in adjusting his dress, then first discovers he has been robbed. Those who give preference to this mode of *do*, are of the secondary sort of thieves, not at all to be considered clever ; they mostly wear short jackets, (at least one of them) the better to effectuate escape by running, the cloth being made smooth, if not slippery, with grease, &c. their operations seldom commence until dusk; they never attack other than *single* persons; and the fall of the year, is the most prolific in this sort of crime.

If this be not " foot-pad robbery," I know not what is; the only difference seems to lie in that robber who *demands* the property in one case, in the other he takes it *without asking.* The genuine decent pickpocket, who does the trick in a neat way, deems himself insulted in being classed with those, as well as with the following description of street robbers: He decries the use of violence upon the person robbed, unless it be in self-defence, and to make his escape.

Women hustle at night, while bestowing their unasked for caresses, adroitly entering your pockets should you come in contact with them. A short lass, and a tall or big one, are the best adapted to this business: the former forcibly contending with the latter the promised enjoyment, seizes you round the middle lasciviously, when the business is done neatly; she hands over the things to her companion, who moves off instantly, while the other keeps you in tow until the booty is out of reach, and then she becomes uneasy until she herself is safely out of your sight. But should you charge the watchman with her person, you would not recover the property, and the charge falls to the ground as a matter of course. I have frequently known *both* women brought in and searched, but nothing was found upon them ; in such cases they have a third accomplice, but generally the stolen things have been deposited in some *nook* or *corner* conveniently situated near where the transaction took place—such as the interstices of window shutters, for bank notes ; or the broken corner of the same,—holes are dug in the mortar of walls for the express purpose,— very often upon the ledges where window-shutters are stowed away by day. Such are the contrivances of those wretches who prowl the streets to take advantage of silly men.

Never suffer a watchman to go out *alone*, after he has heard the charge, in which the *scene of action* is of course pointed out : he would *take care* of the property himself ; and you might ascertain that he had met with it, by his becoming extremely jolly in his answers, not to say impudent,—among other things, affecting to doubt "whether you ever had so much about you."

TRIPPING UP, (BY THE *PADS*)

Is the next degree of street depredation, and is performed either with a stick, which is thrust

between the legs, or by kicking up the heels of
the party. A little more violent still, is the mode
of KNOCKING DOWN, with the fist, or a bludgeon.
This latter is seldom or ever heard of in our *streets*,
but both are practised at the out-skirts, leading to the adjacent towns. So strong and active
are the patrol at present, that robberies never
occur at the hours of *their* being on the watch.

Boys will throw themselves down flat before
persons they design to make prey of; the accomplice pressing forward from behind, precipi-
tates you over the former, who, in rising up draws
out your watch with the utmost facility. Or you
may be *eased* of your money with as little difficulty, while thus bent down, let the breeches
be so ever tight.

At the moment we were going to press with
this sheet, (March 22, 1818,) three Urchins,
attacked some ladies in Holborn, who waited
the drawing up of a Hampstead stage (which
takes place near the house of our publisher.)
Although apparently little rogues, they brought
their victims to the ground; and, but for
timely interposition, or, from immature skill,
would have robbed the three ladies. The time,
was *past dusk*.

When women slip down in the street, or faint away, I would advise you to think twice before you lend your assistance ; for, although she may turn out that which she *appears to be* (a very respectable person), yet the thieves are so numerous, and constantly upon the alert, that it is a thousand to one, but you get *done* in some way or other : it happens sometimes, that the lady herself *draws* you, having been pushed down, or tripped up by one of her own fellows ; also, these sort of women know how to run plump against you, as if they had been killed by the collision, and down they go !

Should a lady under your own protection fall or faint, in the streets, (your wife for instance) take good care what persons (women or men) lend their assistance : it is a great chance but they will be upon the *do*, probably for the first time in their lives.

We just now hear of a gentleman who has found occasion to come home alone, three times a week from Homerton, at very late hours, (sometimes an hour after the patrol went off duty) without any interruption whatever; and this, although he always traversed the garden-lanes, and crossed over the fields, during a great part of the winter, without other arms than a stick,

E

or any light, natural or artificial, for the greater number of times. The reader is requested not to follow the example, seeing that this gentleman, in addition to much personal courage, was withal reckless of life; and that the well-known *havidge* called "Haggerstone" lies but a short distance from the path. Of this place it is a sufficient character to tell, that the constables dare not enter it, to execute a warrant, in the usual way by two or three, but are compelled to augment their numbers, in order to overcome a stout repulse; and yet the place cannot muster above forty men; about a third of whom may deserve a *middling* good character.

Notwithstanding this anecdote, which we know to be fact, it is not to be denied, that numerous offences of these latter descriptions take place all round London, which are never made public, for various reasons. Of these, the chiefest are the dislike people have to be considered keepers of late hours; add to this the trouble and anxiety of prosecutions, the incipient proceedings upon which are by no means rendered palatable to the prosecutor's taste; the desire in most people to keep out of public notice (though sought after by so many others), and we have accounted for the impunity a great number of offenders enjoy.

When the victim is *floored*, imprecations and oaths, and threats of vengeance, in case of resistance, immediately follow, accompanied by the most active search for the property, while they cover his mouth, kneel on his body, or beat him, as the case seems to them to require. The voice is generally in an under tone, or a kind of vociferated whisper; and many of these fellows are really so savage, that they will inflict further punishment if dissatisfied with the booty they may find.

N. B. The reader, especially if he be a stranger to the ways of town, should not ramble about in lanes, or bye-ways, especially at dusk; and the more so, if he is conscious his appearance is such as to promise an easy conquest, or a good booty. Therefore, people should never carry *much property*, in such situations, nor seem puzzled at the route they should take, nor *show* their distrust at the appearance of the rogues, but stare them in the face.

Now as to these, and all personal robberies, *out of doors,* I would advise a sort of knowing circumspection, on which I made some remarks before. Suppose, for a moment, that you were to bustle through the crowd in the streets, shoving about the people; thus, in order to avoid the pickpockets, assuming yourself to be one, to all external appearance? It is not probable you would be attacked by them, upon the old and sure principle, that *dog* will not eat *dog*. So if you stare them well in the face (not sheepishly), eye them downwards, *twig* the shabbiest part of their dies ,—and. if a *row* is begun, you join in the phrases used, as " go it ;" " *now*, d—n his eyes ;" " w at are *you* at ?" " now for it ;" " go it my jumbo !" or, whatever may be said upon the occasion, you would certainly increase. the chances of getting clear. This is what I always repeat. " The *chances* only of getting clear of their clutches" are increased by following these precautions ; for no one can be at a certainty ; as I have known a police officer (Handcock of " Hatton Garden," five years ago) to be stopped and robbed on the highway, when well-armed, and a magistrate who had his pocket picked at the theatre.

As one test of the truth of what I have said, you will invariably discover in the person whose pocket has been picked *while walking singly*, something that points him out as a proper object .of attack : he is easily to be found out as an *unknowing* one ; he is either a silly looking chap, or an unwieldy one, or a new comer. In making this distinction of walking *singly*, I beg to claim the full force of the word; for, as to picking pockets in a crowd, it is quite a different sort of matter,—there, every body goes to wreck. The reader of any discernment, then, will see the propriety of keeping out of crowds; for in them nothing can help him, but strength to get away as soon as possible; and that will be scarcely in his power, if he is well wedged in by eight or ten desperadoes.

Need a word be said of the necessity of keeping the handkerchief concealed, if you mean to preserve it? An outside pocket, in which the handkerchief is visible, is sure to part with its contents at noon-day, even, though you should not walk half the length of the Strand. That circumstance would be most likely to bring its owner into further trouble; as so careless a mode of placing the handkerchief marks him out for one of the *unknowing* ones, he would be followed and further pilfered, as certainly as that he has a nose.

Walking, from the time of dusk to that of the patrols coming on duty, a little before or a little after, is more replete with danger as the *times* are worse. Men who only rob occasionally are thereby driven to desperation; and they then sally forth to commit depredations on the persons of

the unwary, which we, upon mature reflection,
(after detection of the offenders) frequently
consider to partake in a small degree of insanity.
Their necessities blind their judgments on such
occasions; they mistake the object, and get into
trouble, from which they are released only by a
hempen habeas corpus. Such a mistake may be
compared to the old story of " catching a tartar."

Therefore, it is advisable, to keep a good look
out, and especially avoid fellows who are running
hard, or who follow you step by step for any
length of way. Pull up all at once, regard the
motions of the foe, and resolve upon a stout resistance, if you are likely to obtain help in *a minute's* space, by calling out while you parry the
blows, or the endeavour to get you down. If
help is not at hand, so as to come up to your
assistance in that time, you had better give it in
with a good grace, and submit to your fate; for
they will but increase their brutality as you rise
in your opposition—in case they are not inter-
rupted, or likely to be.

But mark this: provided you make good use
of your lungs, and also make a decent stir before
you get *touched* with hand or stick, I'll *pound*
them to *bolt* in a jiffy; for those sort of gentry
have a maxim, " never to give a chance away ;"

and as they are rank cowards, they, on such an occasions, put a question to themselves, and that is " *Which* is to be off the first ?" since he that remains to the last is likeliest to be taken.

These statements are exemplified often: the robbery of a gentleman in Shepherd and Shepherdess fields by the three bakers (1816), one of whom proposed to murder him, because he made so much noise, is a proof of one part of the above proposition ; for, although the place is much frequented, yet no one was nigh enough to alarm them from their purpose. Another part of the above statement was proved under our own observation while yet we were writing it [January, 1818.] A Mr. F—d was followed from the meeting house in Moorfields along London Wall by two of a gang who inhabit thereabout : they were short and stout ; Mr. F. being a little lame in one leg, gave them good reason to expect an easy conquest, as his appearance did a good booty. At the turning into Basinghall Street, (no one at that moment coming up it) one of the rogues ran up to Mr. F—d, pushed a leg between his, and brought him to the ground ; instantly putting his hand into his waistcoat pocket, he had but just time to extract a few shillings, when his accomplice became alarmed at the vociferations of the gentleman (though he already knelt upon him)—and ran away. They could not be overtaken, nor was the occurrence known beyond the circle of his own friends. It was an operation of about half a minute.

Here it will be noted that the *end of a street* was chosen; and hence it may be concluded that such would be always preferred, even though I did not know that *tactic* before hand. Indeed, it will scarcely be expected that I should adduce instances, or proofs, of any proposition I lay down, seeing that every word comes from actual experience, either personally, or by immediate information from the real actors in the scenes I describe. Well, then, I have to inform you, Reader, that the corner, or opposite the corner of a lane, or other avenue is always fixed upon; and the moment is that in which they come to take a glance down it, to see that it is clear of interruption. Sometimes an accomplice runs on before, to find the turning that will suit the purpose; he then goes into it a yard or two, and turns about just in time to contribute his assistance to the plundering; perhaps to receive into his arms, the victim who has been knocked towards him, and to complete the *flooring* of the unfortunate person.

Few such cases are brought before the magistrates; but I repeat it, they happen oftener than
would readily be supposed. On that account it
is, I have dwelt upon particulars so long, in order
that my readers may learn to avoid the dangers
that thus surround them. To which let me add,
—let them look out sharp upon hearing a whist-
ling or calling, even although the latter should be
but a person's name (man or woman), or the
former, the ingenious imitation of the canary
bird's call. The fag-end of a song is a good
signal sometimes; though the words may not be
appropriate, they convey a meaning previously
agreed upon, and are as intelligible to each other
as Greek to a Greek, or the sign and counter-
sign to the guard that visits a military out-post.

N. B. If two persons are in company, it is the
safest method, at late hours and dangerous places,
to walk at some distance from each other—say
from six to eight yards; it would require double
numbers to attack both at once, besides the
chance there would be of one of you running away
and making a *row*, if both attacks did not take
place simultaneously. Moreover, strangers to
town in particular should be careful not to let
others know what money or valuables they carry
about them; and the town-bred knowing-ones

too, had better profit by the advice, and not submit to be drawn of their secret by the offers of
preposterous wagers, the usual method of coming
at a knowledge of the contents of your pockets.
I verily believe some street robberies proceed
from this very cause, and are perpetrated by the
friends, or companions of the sufferers themselves, who probably commit no other offence
during their lives. This last is, to be sure, a
mere supposition, but I could not otherwise account for three or four such robberies that have
been circumstantially detailed to me; but it is
much more probable that a person thus excited
to the commission of crime, would continue in
the same course until the hour of detection arrived.

Although we again disclaim to treat of those
offences and evils that have ceased, yet we should
be guilty of a dereliction of duty were we to omit
noticing the

HIGHWAYMEN,

That upon very rare occasions, start up in the
neighbourhood of this metropolis. Indeed, so
seldom are they now heard of compared to what

they were formerly, that the mention of this offence will appear mere *Bagatelle* to most of our
readers after all the apologies we can offer.   It
was a mistaken notion of Mr. Barrington, that
they receive intelligence from the ostlers and other
attendants at inns, or introduced themselves into
the company of travellers, of whom they wormed
out the secret of their property, its amount, and
the hour they meant to take the road, &c.
Whatever might have once been the case, I will
venture to say no such thing has happened within forty years last past.

No, no, they chance it, when they *do* go out.
Else how came Joe Haines to attack the Bow
Street officers, in the Green Lanes ?   If he had
intelligence at all of three Traps being in the post-
chaise he made precious bad use of it.   He was
shot in the thigh, and afterwards taken and
hanged in chains.   That took place twenty-one
years ago ; and since that time we have heard of
about four highwaymen only ; the most promi-
nent of which was the robbery of the Leeds mail
by Huffey White; and another, nearer home, of a
Young City Traveller who having lost his money
at Newmarket races, stopped some people on
Finchley Common, was pursued by the horse

patrol [Highgate to Barnett] as far as Kentish-town, where he was taken.

N. B. Persons who travel with a good deal of property, if they mean to preserve it, should provide fire arms, at all events, taking care that they are in primest order for firing; for it will be an easy matter to foresee, that a flash in the pan would occasion your certain death. No time remains for priming when a desperate fellow holds a pistol at your head. You should also make up your mind to *do execution*, if put to the test : dalliance with edge tools in such cases would be fatal. To this mistaken notion Mr. Fryer sacrificed his life in White Conduit fields (1796) : having *thrown out his tuck*, and failing to *use* it, the foot-pad shot him dead ! This is a practical lesson for you, even though I did not know before hand what was likely to take place, in almost every possible extremity.

SHARPERS,

Such as GAMBLERS, RING-DROPPERS and MONEY-DROPPERS, SETTERS or Trappers, Crimps (for sea or land service,) Impostors, and Swindlers,

come next under consideration in the order here
set down ; being a numerous and pernicious
annoyance to all persons walking the streets,
where they generally pick up your acquaintance,
or at the public house, at which you may turn in,
to take refreshment. .

The propensity to gambling pervades the entire
population of the north of England; and most
Welchmen settle the commonest disputes that
occur by wager, offering to lay more money upon
one senseless dispute than perhaps ever belonged
to their whole family at any one time. Those are
denominated

WAGERING KIDDIES.

In the city, where a person meaning to ridicule
the practice, or to give an elucidation of it, ob-
served, That laying of wagers were attempts to
come at the money of others by undue, but ex-
cusable, means. Upon which he entertained
the following opinions, in the form of aphorisms :

A wager well layed is already half won.
Wagers are not layed to be lost :
For if lost, they are not to be paid.
So, if the decision goes against you, still
The money must not be paid, but

Payment must be talked off; if that will not do,
————-quarrelled off; if that won't do,
————-fought off.

Such is a tolerably fair account of many men, some of respectable occupations in life, but who are nevertheless Sharpers in the fullest sense of the word,—who will even boast of the money they win at laying *quirkish* bets. The intention is, to take in the unwary, and is not a bit better than picking of pockets or purloining in a dwelling-house. What appears the most galling part of the business to me is, that those men brag of their honesty, and look down upon their poorer, but more upright neigbbour, with disdain. They are called upon juries to try their fellow (criminals?) creatures, and many among us think them *competent* judges of what is a proper verdict in all cases but their own.

For a great number of years that a friend of mine frequented the coffee-houses, so called, round Covent Garden, he witnessed a nightly and daily struggle to take money out of each others' pockets by dint of this deep laid trickery. At one of them, where the most doltish set in the world meet, a couple of Welchmen from *the city*, came in to see what could be *done* in their own way. One of them eggs on the other to

begin some favourite subject; which happened
to be the exact words of a verdict upon a trial at
the Old Bailey that day. As is usual with a
stupid set, and was expected by the speaker, one
contradicts what was asserted, and the rest join
in the contradiction. A wager is offered, and
laid; it is doubled and doubled, and laid with
all who choose to say *done!* " Who is to decide,
look you?" asked the Welch wagering kiddy.

" Who! why any respectable man who heard
it to be sure;" answered a glum old fellow, who
did not so much relish the wordy contest as the
smell of the *blue mark*, (as they call a bowl of
punch) which accompanied every wager for money.

This mode of deciding was greeted as just by
the other wagering kiddies, and agreed to by
the Welch one, who told them he could " show
them one of the jury presently. Who, now,
look you! do you think was the foreman, then,
upon that trial? Ah! you shall find I knows as
much as all of you about things. Now, I will
bet you a blue mark and five pounds I find
the foreman in this neighbourhood."—" This
was too bad," they said; and began to smell a rat.

Our Welchman resumed, " ah, it is too bad for
you. What do you think of Mr. Jenkin James,
Esquire, here?"

His companion, the other Welchman had indeed been that foreman; and had given the verdict in a peculiar manner—whether with any design upon the *gentlemen* of this room is too much
to say. Some of them called it a *do;* and a
broad faced north countryman, wanted to prove
metaphysically that the decision was against
justice. But that attempt did not succeed.
This was a robbery, and nothing else.

The same friend being at a celebrated betting-
house a few nights before this sheet went to press,
was witness to the most barefaced robbery of five
pounds,—under the semblance of a *wager,* that
ever was committed by foot-pad or highway man !
At the famous trotting-house in ———Moorfields,
one of the company, who was unusually *opaque,*
from the use of grog, was set upon by another,
more *transparent* than himself, to play at
draughts ; not with himself, for he could not
play, but with another man, who came in *a little
before him.* It was to no purpose the groggy
man cried off—pleaded his " inability,--that he
was *too ripe* to lay wagers," crying " Peter, I
will lay with you to-morrow, when I know more
of my man !" Oh, no ! this was the only thing
that would not do; and the gentleman was
bothered into the deposit of his money to play

with one who was *a dead nail!* A plant! Need
the reader be told how the bull ran? It was a
close rub.

We have given these as two gross instances.
There are others more subtle; and some others
that are *meant to be lost*,—in order to draw you
on'; and a few that are fair, but depend upon
judgment. For instance, at the house in Middle
row, Holborn, you shall find of a day half a
dozen bets depending on the number of coaches
which shall go up or go down the street in a given
time; sometimes they are laid on the gross
amount of their whole numbers affixed on the
doors. Others again wager on the prevalence of
grey horses, or black ones, &c. Judgment may
be brought in aid of the wagering kiddies, even
in these foolish bets; for about play-going time
(six o'clock) more coaches go up than down, of
course more amount in numbers will go that way,
and more grey horses.

CARDS.

Such is the least blameable species of gambling!
What must be those of blacker hue? Notwithstanding the law, concerning low games at public
houses, cards are used in about one-fourth of

them throughout the year. Strolling into an
Inn yard in Whitechapel a few days ago, to pick
up information for this book, I walked into the
"tap-room," to notice the manœuvres upon the
arrival of a coach,—then expected. Here presently came in a horse-keeper, the ostler, a waiter,
and a hanger-on, whom I knew to be a thief,
from a cut in his face, which I noticed particularly when upon his trial once. They called for
the cards, as a thing of course, and played at all-
fours, for porter and small wagers.

While I gave them room to imagine I was such
a fool as to be *touting* the landlady, I had an
eye to the game, in which there was no small
cheating. In order to make friends with the
hanger-on, I called out, in slang, when his ad-
versary rubbed off a chalk too many. My eye!
how he did *open !* "Called him *all* but a gentleman," in such rum style, and offered two to one
upon the game as it now stood, which was accept-
ed by a young countryman, who had been fool-
ishly induced to hold their stakes from the
beginning, which was the first step towards being
taken in. By the way, in putting down again
the chalk, which had been so improperly taken,
our hanger-on extended his little finger in such
a manner as to rub out one of his own chalks;

but all would not do, though the countryman
" *stood it* like bricks and mortar," he won the
odds upon that game, which was too palpably
gone at the moment to be mistaken for *a win.*
Need the reader be told that he lost in the sequel ?
He lost four games " *successfully*" *(successively,)*
" all hand running." I myself tried on the noodle
for a *tizzy* or two : he got the wrong side of the
post there too; and if I had chosen to be *sweet
upon him,* I m'ght have *drawn him something
handsome,* for he was ready *tip ;* but I had better
business in hand, as the others had shortly after,
when the ———————— stage coach drove into the
yard, each man putting his *hand* (of cards) into
his pocket, as he sallied forth. The hanger-on,
however, first taking a survey through the
windows before he went out, and as for me, I was
stagging the whole party ; but can take upon
myself to say nothing was then done ; for had
there been, I should have split and turned
honest, as is usual.

" Do you know him in the new corderoy
jacket ?" asked the tap-keeper of me ; " he with
the large gilt buttons ?"—" I think I have seen him
at play before." I answered, cautiously ; adding I
" wonder what post he fills here ?"—" What *post !*"
echoed the tap-keeper ; " do you not think that

I am as great a fool as you? I wonder why
Mr. S —— lets him hang about here for; there
is one or two other such sometimes."

I did not reply, but continued *to stag* ; which
he perceiving, asked whether I *wanted* any one?
and demanded pardon for making so bold,
" did he not play with me lately a *whole fore-
noon* in Wood Street, at BAGATELLE ?"

I gave him to understand that he *might*; for
I had been out of place, and picked up a few
stray shillings in that way, which came in very
sweet to me, notwithstanding my appearance.

Here he put me upon an examination: "Could
I *draw* the nine ? Make sure of any hole once
out of twice? Could I *top* forty once out of
three goes ?" To all which I answered modest-
ly in the affirmative; upon which he chuckled
a good deal; proposed that I should act the
novice to-morrow at *the board*, until something
handsome was betted, and that he and me would
make a good thing of it. Finally, we parted,
with a promise to meet again, and a repartee
pun : he asked " which do you use, mace or
cue ?" To which I answered that I myself was
mace, but I could come it the *cue*. Here the
bon mot consists in turning the tap-keeper's noun
mace into the verb *to mace*, or cheat.

In the room which he pointed out to me, I saw no Bagatelle board, so took the liberty to make enquiry after it. Some low fellows had it in the kitchen, to which I repaired; but this room being immediately under the publican's eye, he' never permits them to play for more than a pint of porter, and makes no little parade of the regulation,—though I was convinced he himself would be the first to break through it. He afterwards removed the board into the parlour, where some one or other continued to play from noon to midnight, as I afterwards found.

Going towards Holborn I looked into three places where the same *game* was playing; and took the liberty of looking in upon them again after business was over, and found they had all been as actively employed, pretty nigh, as that one in Wood Street.

By actual reckoning I have found these boards to average the amount of liquor lost and won at them, at something less than three shillings per hour, when they are going; and it is no unusual thing to find them engaged three or four deep; disputes often arising for the next turn or go. Now as nine of these boards are kept in Farringdon Ward alone, I calculate there are one hundred and eight in *the city*, and not less than four

hundred and fifty within the Bills of Mortality ;
making, for the whole of *London*, an average loss
(for liquors only) of four hundred and five pounds
a day, estimating each to be occupied only six
hours.   As all these have been taken at estimates
too low for the actual state of things, we may
correctly set the amount down at the round sum of
five hundred pounds a day, without saying a
word of the *dry money*, which may, we can safely
conjecture, be as much more ; or a total of one
thousand pound daily for the gratification of a
game at once new and fascinating.   So much for
La Bagatelle, at which novices do frequently
win large *numbers*, and the best players are sometimes foiled.   For my part I never lost *any thing*
at it ; and in my last play won *every thing*.
But it is no less pernicious to the stranger, who
is sure to be *done*, either by *booty* or *playing off*.
Therefore it is, I warn my readers to keep clear
from invitations to, even " one roll up of the
balls," for ever so small a wager ; for, as I am not
now *playing*, but *writing* for the good of the
uninformed,   I should not perform my duty
(I am told) if I did not *come out* with every precaution and advice in my power ; and I will add,
if they are not cured by my exposition of the

danger they run, I will play any one of them to-morrow, ——— and beat him.

Draughts are more generally in use: and they are in like manner followed with enthusiasm by the votaries of Mercury, that president of pur-loining, among the ancients. So intense are the players at this stupid game, that you may see a couple of decent men, who deserve a better occupation, bestowing the utmost extension of their faculties upon the upshot of a game that deserves, nor shall receive from me other than the bitterest execration, because it is the grave of thought, the extinguisher of every generous sense. Do men meet together to shut their minds up upon a move of timber? and then, when the *game* is over, start up as if awaked out of a sleep to join in the jovialities of the evening? After " pushing about the wooden gods," as Johnny Bee used to call them, can they descend to con-verse with us mortals? No!

But they are not less the means of taking money (or money in the shape of *drink*) out of your pockets. It is the common practice to *let you in*; if you intermeddle, or give your advice (for novices can see *a move* which the experienced player cannot). *Verbum sat.* Should you bet or play, you are *done*.

Next to draughts, in a general way, is back-gammon, a game of *science indeed,* as well as of *luck.* Although you cannot play, you may bet; but if you do you are *done.* The moment the bets are made superior to the stakes at play, the game is sold. Sold! Even in the most respectable looking company, you are done out of your bet to a dead certainty.

Those, with dominos, are the only games *at play,* in a general way, to which the untaught, unpractised visitor to our Metropolis is exposed. Other and more ardent trials await the *man of money,* and of warm, generous feelings, who thinks every one he meets as honest as himself. Faro, Rouge et Noir, E. O. Vingt-une, Hazard, are the *high-cut* games of those who attack the vitals of an hereditary estate, or the peace of a family, long ennobled by *acts* of nobleness, which royalty cannot enhance by the fictitious addition of its ribbons, its smiles, or the laying on of a sword; much less by writing on a piece of paper or parchment the *word* BARON, VISCOUNT, or EARL! What less was Mr. P—— before he was lord B—! how was his state altered by being created Earl of M——?

Lately, a general *blow up* hath taken place of nearly all the *do's* at the West end of the town,

by means of a most *ill-written* poem, the stanzas
of which have served as a kind of pegs upon which
to hang the *notes*. The consequence has been,
that new and yet unpractised methods are daily
resorted to, of which we will apprise our readers
by and by, whereby to come at the money of the
unsuspecting stranger. We think the poet has
no more rhyme than we have sense; we know
more than he does of the things he describes; and
some things of which he appears to know nothing.
We allude to "*the Greeks*," a poem.

What signifies his telling the public about the
two sevens (77) in Jermyn Street, or the same
quaint description of the feverish *do*. (77) in Pall
Mall? the so-called subscription houses! Or indeed, any house or person, if he describes not the
mode in which the novice in town is done out of
his money? *Names* and *places* have changed in
nine months, wonderfully. To be sure, those
remain; they remain *known;* whereas they were
antecedently known only to a few (the *chosen*
few) black legs. But a question arises in our
minds—why did he *suppress* every mention of
the three houses next the palace gate? or the
tree at the opposite corner, which, like a *will-o'-
the-wisp*, is now up, now down, now in, now out?
He is shrewdly suspected by many of interested-

ness, who could thus pass over those who, equally
in flagrante delictu, were practising the same
frauds as their neighbours. *The poet* did not
mention the house in Bury Street, as he ought,
nor the name of Oldfield, with proper discrimination, to be understood as guarding the *unpractised* stranger from entering his house. He could
not be aware, indeed, of the subsequent Bow
Street examination, at which even the watchmen
could *come out* with so much intelligence; nor
of the four *new* establishments in Pall Mall with
the oval panes, where every thing is affected to
be done fair and above board.

Furthermore, of what use is the mention of a
Smith, or a Hewetson! They can change names
as well as appearances and residence; and the
unpractised in the ways of town (and indeed, the
most practised) shall be deceived by the glitter-
ing external of houses and persons, which change
with *the seasons* their Proteus form! It is the
practices, the arts, and delusions resorted to,
which constitute the danger; and the more
finesse that is used, the more is the chance increased of your falling a victim to the snares laid
out for your destruction.

How, or in what way, it came to be known,
remains yet to be developed, that a young gen-

tleman from Oxford, in going home to spend the
vacation, took up his residence at a house in the
city, totally out of the verge of all gambling.
Probably he was induced to adopt that house,
as well from its vicinity to the mail-coach office,
as its having been the usual residence of his late
father in town, and consequently, that the most
respectable mercantile gentlemen from the north
put up at.   Hither, however, he must have been
traced; for here, on the very day of his coming,
a very dashing blade of the *first water*, made his
appearance, and took up his residence; although
he was rather *outré cela*, yet his driving a stilish
gig and commanding a groom, could be no objection to give him the common courtesies of the ——
and ——.   At the first interview with the young
gentleman, who had a previous disposition *for
play*, the wily gambler (for so he turned out to
be) warmed himself into his esteem by dint of
face, a goodly person much beyond the common
cut, and the knowledge of several esteemed gra-
duates, from whom he had so lately parted at the
university.

   " By G——, Sir, you shall dine with me," exclaimed the fine fellow : " four o'clock, say you !"
" Make it five. I have two humdrum acquaintance
at that hour upon a *Yes* and *No* business, so you

shall dine with me. Between you and me *the occasion* deserves a damned good dinner; however, of that more anon."

Who would not concede *an hour* upon such an *occasion!* A good dinner, an agreeable companion, and two dull friends to give audience to all you may utter, could not be unacceptable to a young gentleman full of spirit, who was almost alone, except when visited by the lawyers concerning the family property which, by the deaths of his elder brother and father, had devolved upon him to manage.

Before they sit down to dinner, the reader must be told that the dashing blade of the stilish gig and groom was a black leg! His two humdrum acquaintance, as he termed them, were likewise two sharpers from the same hot bed of insidious robbery—St. James's. And he was under the necessity of postponing the dinner hour, that he might have time to send for them; as probably they were *then in bed!* And even when they came, another couple were sent for, the booty was expected to be so great!

The dinner over, our party of four resolved on a game at whist, and ordered a couple of packs of cards. But no: a person in the house knew one of the couple, who had come in, to have been

dealer at a *Rouge et Noir* table, and now belonged to a *Bank*, which played all comers, at "*the
two sevens.*" Cards were accordingly refused,
on some genteel pretence, and the refusal would
no doubt have thrown our spark into a fit of madness, (if we may judge by his present behaviour)
but from the consolation of a promise, that to-
morrow cards would be provided. During this
paroxysm he paid the bill for dinner and wine,
with an air which bespoke utter indifference for
the sum total.

Good wine with good company, quickly digest
a good dinner, and make the minutes roll merrily
away. No time seemed to have elapsed since
dinner, when that harbinger of ill-news, the
waiter entered, with the appalling information
that the horses were putting to; but there was
still a good quarter of an hour to spare.

"A quarter of an hour!" exclaimed the
Leg: "damnation! What horses?"

"Mail, Sir!" smirkingly replied waiter.

"I have taken my place, and must depart.
You may recollect I told you yesterday I should
go the moment my business was finished: the
fortunate postponement of dinner, enabled me
happily to complete the negociation I was upon,"
Said Mr. B—d, the intended dupe; and he did

set off, notwithstanding the pressing intreaties of the gallant *leg* and his two companions. Their arguments wanted logic. "*Cui bono?*" asked he, inwardly; and when he found the answer to be "a game at Whist, to-morrow evening," and the consequent delay of two days in setting out, he came to his conclusion, which nothing could move.

He went; and the two "dull friends," went *their way*. But our *leg* expected two more of the club to look in, and did not choose to wait and hear their reproaches and vexatious remarks, which he knew would follow the disappointment and expences they underwent; so whilst his groom was "putting to" he wrote the note, of which the following is a copy :—

"H.

"I am off from here : 'tis all up, the bird (*pigeon !*) is flown. The blo—y b—r B—d had taken his place in the mail, and would go.

Your's, S."

This he *wafered* up, and left with the waiter; but the wafer was wet, which, as he let a significant word drop that excited much talk, the waiter resolved to open. On jumping into his gig, he incautiously ejaculated to his groom, in tones of discontent, "no *do*, by G—!" Such an expression "let the cat out of the bag" with a vengeance;

it showed the cloven foot, and the attempt to fleece this young gentleman stood as much exposed as if the parties had been at confession.

Will ye not learn, incautious youth! from this real and veritable narration, that no pains or expence are spared to intrap you in the toils of the destroyer? That men combine their purses and talents to defraud you of your patrimony; no time, place, distance, or combination, being an obstacle to the pursuit of their object. Did we not hear, with agony, the disclosures of an equally villanous attempt, at Brighton in Autumn, 1817, of one O'M—ra, (a nine years resident there,) who dispatched *his leg* to London at a great expence to bring back a well-fledged pigeon to be plucked under his own eye? But the scheme failed through accident.

Although we have given instances from high-life, yet the same practices come all the way, by gradations, down to the meanest man that ever had a pound to lose. A party—respectable let us suppose for a moment—meet at a house, respectable enough for your ideas of propriety, to play a fair game at cards. " No high betting !" No. But then, into such a party, however upright may be the leading persons, some one or more black sheep is likely to show his front. *4* leg, as arrant a black leg, as ever entered the purlieus of St. James's, may be found in St. Paul's church yard; and so far as leg-ism (cheating) goes, they have as many tricks at the one as at the other place.

If a man is to be *done*, what signifies it to him, whether that be by a game at vulgar *put*, or the more elegant (because frenchified) *Rouge et Noir, et tous les deux?* What, if he gambles his all, whether it amounts to hundreds, or thousands, or tens of thousands?

False dice, is a common cheat, of which the game of *roley poley* is but an imitation; but there never was a pair made that by use did not lose their true die or square, and thereby receive a new bias, known only to those who are in the habit of using them.

Of horses and cocks, and the athletic games, we have said nothing: in the first place they are not *London* games; and secondly, we say, bet not at all; upon the most trivial matter they are meant but to decoy and entrap the unwary, who, if a *doubt* arises, is sure to be out-voted in strange company.

See more under the head of Lottery-offices and pretended parsons, lawyers, and doctors.

MONEY-DROPPERS,

Are no other than gamblers, who contrive that
method to *begin play*. It is an almost obsolete
practice; and its twin-cheat, ring-dropping, is
not less disused: Men, now-a-days, manage things
more subtly; both kinds of these *droppers*, too,
vary their mode of proceeding to infinity. " What
is this ?" says the dropper; " my wiggy ! if this is
not a leather purse with money ! Ha ! ha ! ha !
Let's have a look 'at it.'" While he unfolds its
contents, his companion comes up, and claims
his title to a share. " Not you, indeed! replies
the finder, this gentleman was next me; was not
you, Sir ?" To which the countryman assenting,
or, perhaps, insisting upon his priority, the finder
déclares himself no churl in the business, offers to
divide it into three parts, and points out a public
house at which they may share the contents,
and drink over their good luck : talks as they
go of his once sharing in a much larger sum,
with a " stranger, who was honourable :—nothing
like honour !" The found money is counterfeit,
or *screens*, or else *Fleet notes*.

They drink, and fill their grog again; and
should a little rain come on, they improve on that
circumstance, or any other; such as the coming

in of an old friend, whom the finder can barely recognise, but remembers him by piecemeal. La Bagatelle, the draught board, or cards, constantly exhibit the means of staking the easily-acquired property so lately found, but which they cannot divide just now *for want of change.* The countryman bets, and if he loses, is called upon to pay ; if he wins 'tis added to what is *coming to him* out of the purse.

If, after an experiment or two, they discover he has little or no money, they run off, and leave him to answer for the reckoning. But with money, they stick to him until all is gone : if he turns a little restive they abuse him ; if he objects to pay he must fight his man ; if he can do that tolerably well, they all fall on board him, and chase him forth of the house with execrations and coarse epithets. Such are among the latest occurrences of this sort, but they do not average once a year.

Another playful mode is, for butcher's boys or stall-keepers' boys, to place a white metal button in the street, with a string fastened to the eye, both of which are pressed into the dirt. A stranger to the trick, might very naturally stoop to pick up what appears to be a shilling ; but no sooner has his fingers come in contact with the dirt (from which he endeavours to extract it) than the young urchin, who holds the string, draws it up suddenly, and the finder has nothing but dirty fingers for his pains. This is the least guilty trick we shall have to record. The

RING-DROPPERS,

Have more cunning to display in turning their wares into money : the pretending to find *a ring* being the lowest and least profitable exercise of their ingenuity.

It makes a part of the ring-droppers art to *find* things much more valuable than those : the favourite articles are jewellery, such as broaches, earrings, necklaces and the like, made up in a paper parcel, sometimes in a small box, in which is stuck a bill of parcels with high flown descriptions and heavy charges. Proceeding with the dupe nearly as before, the sharper proposes, that as he is not in cash, he will willingly relinquish his share for a small proportion of the amount set down in the fictitious bill of parcels; and if you pay him one pound in ten of that amount, you are *done*. The *diamonds* are paste, the *pearls* are the eyes of fish, the *gold* is polished brass, gilt.

This mode, however, and that of picking up a gold ring, close at the feet of a young servant

girl, is very little used. "Is this your ring,
young woman? Let me see your finger; if it is
I shall find a mark there. Well! I'll declare it's
good gold; don't you see the stamp?" says the
dropper; and then he proceeds to inveigle her
into a purchase. But the whole concern cannot
amount to more than three or four shillings, and
is really too shabby to detain the reader upon any
longer.

KIDNAPPERS, FALSE ACCUSERS, TRAPPERS, AND CRIMPS,

Have much altered their plans of operations
within these very few years; for instance, the
last mentioned have entirely disappeared since
the year 1796; being put down by dint of
law, and the little necessity there was for
their services, when the government adopted the
plan of recruiting the army out of the militia.
That department of crimping which applied itself to the land service, then, being abrogated
and done away, we have only to notice that which
is now practised with regard to seamen. The
East India company contract with Crimps for a
supply of sailors to navigate their ships out and
home; these are, for the most part Jews, who have
made advances to the sailors of money *(very*

small sums), clothes, victuals and lodgings;—
every article being charged extravagantly high.
The poor fellows are accordingly placed under
a sort of *espionage*, if not close confinement, till
the ship is ready to receive them; and then they
are conducted on board at Gravesend, by the
Crimp and assistants, and a receipt taken for them.

In this process there is nothing very frightful:
the men want berths, and the Crimp wants to be
sure of his men: the grand *do* is in seamen receiving any thing but money of the Crimp; it is
in watches, buckles, hats, and jackets that the
robbery is committed. And in the victuals,—
foh! the whole is barefaced unblushing robbery. With the same view of doing the unwary
poor fellows, these Crimps get hold of their
" TICKETS" as soon as they come on shore, upon
which they make advances of watches, jewellery
and such stuff, to about one twentieth of the
amount. Not only is this the case in London,
but at all the outports it is practised to a very
great extent, in war-time particularly. Portsmouth
was the seat of unheard-of villainies, and rapid
fortunes, during the long war that has just been
brought to a close.

Happy would it be for poor Jack, were this
all: he is sometimes brought in indebted to the

Crimp to a large nominal amount, by what is called a long-shore attorney, or more appropriately, a black shark, and thrown into jail !!! There he lies until his *body* is wanted, and then the Incarcerator negotiates with him for his liberty, to be permitted to enter on board again. Seamen should take care of their tickets and discharges, though they spend all their money; but if he wants a bit of lark, why not have it with his relations and friends, in his own native place, to which a stage coach would carry him in a day or two, at the rate of ten knots an hour? Advice that ought not to be thrown away at any time, much less during war.

The same class in society, who thus entrap the incautious sailor, are not likely to be compunctuous in taking in the lands-man. One of their chief moves at this game is to charge an innocent person with a crime; first by inuendo, if in-doors at a public house, and then direct, provided they have there a good assemblage of their fellows. These will swear to any thing that may be suggested by their spokesman; and it is best to rebut their most insignificant impertinencies at the outset, and to shew the proper indignation consistently with your character: If you once evince symptoms of fear, standing silently horror-struck,

at the preposterousness of the imputation, they
repeat the blow with redoubled force, and you are
lost, at least your money; for it is to obtain
your money that the charge is made.

Others still lower walk up to gentlemen in the
streets, and accuse them of robbery, or of unnatural crime; of having debauched his wife or
sister, or getting a girl with child—especially if
they know your name. Some years ago a woman
accused a noble lord of having robbed her of a
fifty pound note, and he was tried at the Old
Bailey for it; but she was immediately convicted
of perjury, and transported. Much later, one
Ann Radford accused a person of murdering
another man in her presence; but the latter ap-
pearing in court, staggered belief of her evidence:
she too was convicted, like the former, and about
the time we are writing, may have reached her
place of destination, Botany Bay. Both these
women were postitutes; but the latter was a
country occurrence.

A fellow in the ——— regiment of foot guards,
whose nick name, Nancy Cooper, designates his
character, (as it was considered by the givers),
accused a gentleman in the Strand of a beastly
offence, said to have been perpetrated in St.
James's Park. Struck dumb at the heinousness

of the charge, the accused gentleman complied
with the demand of giving what money he had
about him ; but immediately after was · advised
to prosecute, which he did most effectually, for
Nancy was hanged at the Old Bailey.

Women of the town will walk up to one whom
they think they can easily astonish, with their
stays stuffed out with rags (perhaps), and remind-
ing him of certain foolish familiarities, in which
he has indulged, persuade him by all the tokens
in her power, that he is the father of the child of
which she is *now* pregnant. [An indisputable
fact.] Here she enlarges her tale pitifully, with
an allusion to her helpless state and want of
money ; next touching upon the hardness of
parish officers, and that with a little assistance
she shall be able to lie-in without applying to
them, or swearing the child, which she hopes
may die ! and herself too. Asks him whether
he would advise her to get *relieved* at the ad-
vertised lying-in houses—such as the " Blue
Lamp" in London House-yard ;—or, deeper still,
she invites him to procure abortion medicines :
should he consent, he is a ruined man. A noble
lord (T——d) was safely robbed in this way so
lately as this winter, 1817.

After using these topics, she asks directly for

the money he may have about him ? Hectors and
bullies, not a little, and insists upon his coming
to see her ; or that otherwise she shall come and
see him in a different sort of way. At whatever stage of this boisterous meeting he *bleeds*
the least sum of money probable for the occasion,
she is always ever after sticking in his skirts : if
the silly man takes fright, and is afraid of being
discovered, she brings a companion, and they together bully him out of his money at proper intervals,—perhaps, in a state bordering on distraction, they obtain a promise of marriage ! I leave
the reader to contemplate the effects of such an
union, on his purse, and peace of mind.

Those of which we have spoken, are accusations
without any foundation, there are other and
blacker kinds of criminal charges, made against
individuals, that have *some* ground-work to build
charges upon ; but which becomes, nevertheless,
more atrocious as the perpetrators have twice
double objects in view, viz. the commission of
crime, the detection, the death of the culprit, and
payment for their villainy. Of these we shall
hereafter speak, under their modern and most
appropriate title of BLOOD HOUNDS, which the
reader is desired to see !

Every false accusation goes to the utter extinction of character, they include the fear of imprisonment, and nearly all aim at the life of the accused ; which there is too good reason to believe they sometimes take away, inasmuch as having once ventured to broach the subject there · is no retreat left them. In all cases of false accusation or entrapment, the accusers generally prove too much ; acting always with indecent eagerness they overshoot their mark.

PRETENDED OFFICERS.

Seeing the success which has attended the depredations of officers bearing his majesty's staff— as Vaughan, Brock, Pelham, Johnson and others, many an old thief assumes the garb and authority of such, in order the better to carry on their own, or their accomplices' robberies. This is usually done at night, by ordering off, peremptorily, any casual passenger, or other person, who may be upon the watch, while the *business* is carrying on. At other times, small thieves get about among groups of people, particularly on Saturday night ; and one crying out " be off," " go home," " come, come, I'll have no more of this !" the people show their spirit by reprobating such conduct ; when the accomplice pretends

to take part and carney with them; and hereupon
in the way to the gin shop, while there, or at
coming out, they purloin meat, halfpence, or if
the incautious novice produces his purse, they
prefer that, and its scanty contents.

I one Saturday night saw a fellow at this game
in Whitecross Street, and wishing to be *in it*, I
got into a lot of about a dozen old women, every
one of them more or less *snuffy*, but they were
purloined of pieces of meat by the shabby fellow,
who declared himself an officer, "and talked
about his authority;" but he was below my
" cut," and I blinked him, as there was no one
there worth " *doing.*" Well pleased was I to see
a little man step up to him, and after demanding
what *authority* he meant, squared at him,—
took him a *topper*, and a *breast-cut ;* and afterwards, with the assistance of the patrol, he was
conveyed to the watch house in Bunhill Row.
Here he was *frisked* of his eatables, and stood
the gammon well as ever I saw ; but he got clear
off, because has was known to two of the Wor-
ship Street Traps, who were in attendance there;
and they broiled the stolen mutton, while the
gentleman who had *fibbed* him was fined a half
gallon for his interference. This mutton-thief
turned out to be a Nose to one of these officers,

and that was reason enough for getting off *easy*. He that very blessed night, in my own hearing, split upon *Bill-Bill* of Golden Lane ; who only escaped the sessions by reason of the Nose having called too late upon the officer ; which latter (his wife declared) got up, and had been gone out ever since five o'clock (in the afternoon), " because the house was too hot to hold him.".

Should a " novice in town," ramble into a public house, late in the evening, if it be not very respectable (and that does not matter, at all times) he may have one or two set upon him, pretending to be officers, ordering him and his party home, in expectation of a treat, but if discovered, pretending to be upon the *lark*. Landlords in general pull with them, because they are *old customers, and do good to a house.*

OF SEARCHING.

In cases where a party accused *stands search*, articles are passed into possession of the searched, as suits the purpose of the searcher. When the lads were taken up on Tower Hill for *smashing*, they had no money about them bad or good until after a kind of second search, when the officer conveyed the base coin into their possession.

Some years before, Mr. B —— of Newgate Street was found intoxicated by the watchman, but his watch could not be found, and the drunkard accused the guardian of the night of having stolen it, to his certain knowledge. Search was made, the watchman was dismantled, but no watch could be found upon either party until the *house* was cleared, and then it was discovered upon the right owner. Very few people believed it had been there all the time : but the highest part of the joke was to follow : the watchman, threatened an action for defamation, and received *five* pounds as a compromise for the *damage* his character sustained from the foulness of the charge !

When Jem Leary underwent his *second* examination for the murder of Clifford, his clasp knife was produced; which was pretended to have been found on *the spot*, but which he on his *first* examination, stated to have lent to the deceased at supper time. Now the deed was not committed with a knife, but a hammer; the accused claimed the knife the moment it was produced, said he had left it at home in the cup-board the same morning,—yet was this clumsy incident received in proof. Leary was *hanged*, and the officer *discharged* for something else.

SMUGGLERS.

Some custom house officers searched G——s and Co., in St. Paul's Church yard, for contraband silk goods, in vain; for which they would be liable to an action for damages, and were threatened with it; but *fortunately* one of them found an old Bandana handkerchief in a dirty-clothes bag, which he could swear to as foreign manufacture. However, the assembled domestics and warehousemen would all have sworn equally positive the handkerchief belonged to neither of them, or their master.

N. B. When premises are entered for a search, the family should divide, and accompany each officer. The same as to personal search, a friend of the accused should be present.

As publicans are liable to the penalties for game, or contraband goods found on their premises, though these should belong to other people, they should be careful for whom they take charge of goods, as they are sometimes left for the purpose of laying information. Tom Minter, the Stretton's Coffee House, Newgate market, was so served — but got clear over it, in the Court of Exchequer ! ! Stopp, of the Queen's head, St. John's Street, had his house searched for silk goods of which some were seized, and the fine, after every plea for moderation, he got over only by paying upwards of a hundred pounds.

INFORMERS.

Informers, who find no real dealers in contraband, are obliged to evince their activity to their employers by *creating* them. They wheedle themselves into the good graces of some unsuspecting Noodle at the Alehouse; generally a drunkard who has good connections in life. Him they stuff up with a great idea of what each other is doing in *the trade ;* for there are always two or even six, seven, or eight frequenting the same house. Having *primed* him in this way, some goods are produced *upon the sly,* a lamentation is set up that such great beauties, and so cheap, cannot find a sale ; how happy many ladies would be only to look at such a shawl, or gentlemen such fine large Bandanas ;—then the Noodle's friends are described, as near as may be, and if he does not open his mouth, a direct offer is made to him, his honesty commended, and if he appear a little *seedy* they *rig* him out. For a space of time, be it more or less, he goes on and prospers for a while, thinks it a fine career to move in, and probably, by his example, induces some other

poor devil, like himself, sometimes much more
respectable than either, to embark in the same
trade. Then comes the tragedy. The informers
are in full possession of the names of all the purchasers, and the whole line of connections go to
wreck. If they mean to go on again in the same
career, they manage to get locked up at a
Spunging house; and then inform against the
Noodle they had first duped, who is brought to
the same place, and the old Informer assumes
the character of the " wolf in sheep's clothing,"
worms him of the remaining names of his customers, and informations are issued and penalties
levied against the whole. Both parties express
their sorrow, that the predicament in which they
were placed should have driven them to such an
act, and they are then at liberty to pursue their
avocations at the same place. The more timid
remove to great distances, even so far as from the
Commercial road turnpike to Cork Street, Picadilly, others only into the city, about Newgate
market, to Aldersgate Street, and such neighbourhoods.

In the summer of 1816, Brown obtained a
list of persons likely to buy silk goods in the
counties of Buckingham, Northampton, and
parts adjacent from a gentleman of high respecta-

bility, with whom he had become acquainted at a dining house in Newgate Street;—my Teddy accordingly undertakes the journey as regularly as ever tradesman went upon his business. Some months elapsed before he could lay his informations; for, getting into the King's Bench, his real creditors kept him there and in Horsemonger Lane, four or five months. However, slow and sure, is a good maxim. Some few at Stoney Stratford were taught a lesson they will not shortly forget to the tune of 200*l.* or 300*l.* each.

N. B. These instances show respectable persons how very careful they ought to be in taking recommendations from their most valuable friends, to pursue a course so likely—more than likely—to turn out as these did. This is called a genteel *do.*

British goods are the highest hoax upon the knowing ones. Shawls, scarfs, elastics, &c. are now made equal to the French, in some instances superior; and will puzzle the learned to find out the difference. In December, 1817, the court of Exchequer was filled with witnesses, the best judges of silk goods in the kingdom, who gave their opinion, like men, that our manufactures beat Monsieur's hollow. The defendants, Harding & Co. were therefore fined only in about a

fortieth part of the penalties incurred, as a compromise. This was a great triumph for the British
manufacturer; but none for those who lived by
hawking about the like goods for foreign, and
selling them as such.

This latter go is more particularly in vogue
with regard to Bandana handkerchiefs, which are
now made to resemble the best Batavia. The
house of P. Johnson & Co. make some heavier
than P. T., even sixteen ounces and a quarter,
though it must be allowed the company's goods
[C. G.] are larger and superior, not being too
high-dressed. However, the British is, and must
be taken, as a very fair substitute for the " real
India."

ARTICLES SMUGGLED.

Of smuggling as well as of smugglers a word
or two may not be amiss. The quantity of foreign spirits so introduced to, and used in London,
is very small : no one can hope to buy that which
pretends to be such, of even tolerable quality ; so
that the apparent saving of a very few shillings
per gallon is counterbalanced by the evil of swal-
lowing a hot, fiery, ill-cleansed, and consequently
ill-flavoured article, made up as it is of spirit obtained from every variety of obnoxious materials.

TEAS and COFFEE, the former particularly, must be bad. For they are such as come under one of these heads,—1. Purloined from the war-houses. 2. Sweepings, 3. Imported from the continent or in American vessels. Now, 1. that which has been secreted about the persons of the workmen and porters, is likely to have acquired a flavour very different from what a delicate taste would expect from pure tea. 2. Sweepings from the holds of Indiamen, as well as the sur-plus sea-stock of officers and men, must lose their virtue by exposure, whatever the appearance may be, besides the contamination of every thing offensive. 3. Teas brought to Europe by fo-reigners, are not, at the beginning, so good as those of our East India Company ; who pick and choose and cull all the best goods of every descrip-tion in India as well as here, leaving to private adventurers, private traders and foreigners the refuse. This must be more particularly the case with tea, because the company buy nineteen twentieths of all that is brought to Canton ; the Dutch, the Swedes, French, and Americans, di-viding the remaining one-twentieth between them.

Such is the sort of tea which, on account of the high duty, is smuggled (in very small quanti-ties) about London.

Coffee that is hawked about is not smuggled as is pretended : it is stolen, or inferior, or jobbed for against other goods.

CANDLES and SOAP are generally as good as the regular trade, sometimes better, and make the single exception in that respect, and as to cheapness, of any smuggled articles, you may perhaps obtain prime moulds at one shilling per doz. less than dipt candles ; and about as much saving may be made upon soap.

PRIVATE DISTILLERIES.

But that species of contraband which is carried on to the largest extent, and is most ruinous to those engaged in it, is the distillation of ardent spirits; at one and the same time, the easiest effected, and the hardest to work at of all the illicit manufactures, as the article is difficult to dispose of when made. For publicans hesitate before they embark in a trade, from the trammels of which they can never be free. The makers and vendors frequently turn round upon their heel, and inform against the purchasers ; upon whom, if they are licensed victuallers, the penalties are treble,—and the exise commissioners seldom relax so much on this as they do upon other offences.

Most private distillers keep pigs; for this reason, that they not only eat up the residue of the
materials, but are also a good cloak in bringing
in and carrying out whatever may be necessary.
The pigs go to Smithfield, fat, and store pigs are
brought back in a little cart. A large basket
containing bladders goes forward and backward,
and the business is now effected with more safety
than ever, as I myself have witnessed. Being out
upon a drinking *spree* with four or five others in
the autumn of 1817, near Chelsea, I saw one of
these carts stop at the door, the driver calling for
a pint of beer, as he descended with a small market basket in his hand. As he did not come into
the room where we were, but went backwards into
a dark kitchen-looking place, my curiosity was
raised, so I watched him through the glass as I
sat on the table: he stooped down, as if conceal-
ing something, and went away in a short time
without speaking to any one; as the landlord
never stirred out of our company, and the pot
boy who served him with the beer had been ordered out by his master to get in the pots. What
was my surprise upon sneaking backwards, to
find he had not drank half of his beer! which
I then recollected he did not pay for, so far as I
could see. He had placed two bladders of spi-

I 3

rits underneath the seat, one of which we *boned*
in the most open way imaginable, before the
landlord's face; while two of them made a bit of
lark with the poor fellow, the others walked off
at a round pace with the bladder of spirits, which
proved double strong, but ill-flavoured.

Drunken men and fools, are said to tell the
truth; so think I. Out of such have I wormed *a*
pretty precious *sight* of information. Out of
three or four facts, and shrewd guesses at something more, I come to the conclusion, that several
of our topping Distillers began with (though
they may not continue) private stills. Every
one has heard of the detection of Mr. L———,
heretofore sheriff of London; add to him two
neighbour distillers who are now at the zenith of
commercial prosperity, but who, nevertheless,
formerly kept the private still going, which formed the nucleus of their respective fortunes. In
the dark recesses of an illicit haunt, was laid the
foundation of those splendid equipages, which
dazzle the drivelling practitioner of a more
honest calling! Ascending from the north door
of Saint Paul's N. N. E. ½ N. (as a sailor
would direct an enquirer) at the rate of five miles
an hour, you shall espy one of them in ten
minutes, over the starboard bow, marked R. near

the forechains; and at fifteen minutes run, 'tis
ten to one but you spy the other right a-head,
while upon the larboard wake her gallant well-
found tender lies at anchor in Carthusian Creek.

Of all smugglers, or pretended smugglers, the
most successful are those termed

BUFFERS, MISTAKENLY CALLED DUFFERS.

Many of them make a good living, one or two
have become rich to my certain knowledge, and
almost all, of them heretofore carried *the pack*
up and down the country at fairs, great markets,
and revels. They are invariably north-country-
men. Jordaine was a Glasgow man, and made
ten thousand pounds by the last mentioned profession, but never *buffed it* in the streets of
London, so far as I ever heard, saw, or believe.

The term buffer is derived from the practice
which once prevailed of carrying Bandanas, Sars-
nets, French stockings, &c. next their shirts; so,
as they were obliged to undress in order to come
at the goods, or in other words to strip to the
skin or buff, they obtained the name of buffers.
When Mr. Barrington did his book, they might,
and probably did, carry their goods always about
them, and show them in the streets; now, however,
they carry on trade in a more genteel manner,

leaving a pack at some public house near where
they mean to ply, to which they invite the unwary passenger.

The chief haunt for the buffers has been for
some years at the back of Saint Olave's church
near Union Hall; for the packmen in London,
though they are not numerous, yet in my night
travels, I have frequently seen five or six at a time
turn in at the Falcon, Falcon Square.

Now these *chaps* are not rogues, in the strict
meaning of the word—they only sell to the *best
advantage*. If they can persuade you an article
is better than it actually is, you have nothing to
complain of—every tradesman will do the same.
The chief objection to them lies in their mode of
operations, and in their overstrained recommendation of their goods. As in every other species of
cheatery, they look out for the unknowing, or
silly, to whom, walking up with a demure phiz,
and interesting air, they announce the pleasing
intelligence that they have on sale (as may suit
your appearance) " an excellent piece of cordu-
roy, just sufficient for a breeches piece,"—or
" some real India muslin, just brought home by
a relation, enough for two gowns, at the price of
one ;" or " what would you think of some beautiful French silk stockings as cheap as cotton,

and ten times as strong? Sir, there are two or
or three pieces of *real* India handkerchiefs, fine
wear, that will last your life-time; and always
look well, never wear out: One is yellow—one
is chocolate,—one is ————.   What a pity!
Only just now I sold a [country] gentleman,—
your size,—a beautiful fine waistcoat piece (de-
scribing the one you wear)—full size, genteel,
fast colours, never wear out, at—what d'ye think?".
(then he starts out with a sum just half its value)
—" Down there, Sir; yes, Sir, at that house with
the grapes out, and chequers on, I'll show you
such things as you never saw. Very well worth
your notice, Sir; no harm done, though you
should not buy. I have a pint of porter there
half drank, just step in and look at them."
Then, part by persuasion, part by force, he hands
along his customer to a dark back room, where
probably he exhibits some really good articles, if
he has a judge of them to deal with, but taking
care to " ring the changes" upon wrapping
them up, on the event of a purchase. The certainty of a " *do*" is no longer problematical.

A master-piece of the game is, where his confederate comes in, and begins a conversation with
his brother buffer. At the first, quite strangers
to each other, the comer-in proposes to withdraw,

through bashfulness, but is *ordered* to stay by
the confederate, perhaps asked to partake of
drink; for all which kindness he seems much
obliged, and expresses his thanks *clumsily*. At
length more emboldened, he introduces a word
or two in favour of the goods, magnifies their
value, recommends a purchase, and all at once
recollects having bought some article or other
he now wears of such another man. The two
knaves join in the description of the man, both
agree in the particulars, and in his character for
honesty, shake hands and drink together.

Not less frequently, real tradesmen, living in
the neighbourhood, who frequent the same house,
good naturedly (or with a worse motive) join in
the recommendation of the article to be sold, and
the delusion is then complete—the stranger is
thus taken in with the aid of those who ought to
be his protectors. Should you ultimately refuse
to purchase, you must put up with a great deal
of abuse, provocations to lay wagers, and to fight,
or go through with the quarrel by contending
against fearful odds. Whatever money you pro-
duce never returns to your pockets again; the
landlord is sure to take part against you, " for the
credit of his house;" and all present will declare
themselves ready to swear that you have perpe-

trated such things as in fact you never once so much as thought of. Think yourself well off if you get away without a black eye; but you must lay your account in a kick of the ——, or tweak by the nose.

N. B. Never suffer yourself to be goaded to purchase any article whatever in the streets: they are invariably cheats who attempt it. The shortest way is to decline the least particle of conversation; and if they place their fingers on your arm to stop your progress—peremptorily bid them "hands off," or if you have sufficient strength, knock them down. Whoever places his hand upon your person in the street has nothing good in view, be it man or woman.

JOBBERS.

JOBBERS of nearly the same description abound, who do not stop people in the street, but ply at public houses, offering for sale tobacco, shoes, coals, candles, and such other heterogeneous articles as they think likely to suit the company then there, or the landlord; which latter generally gets supplied with every article of housekeeping, including meat, poultry, salt, clothes, &c. from such "customers." They pretend to have commissions from respectable houses, whom

they sometimes name, asserting they can pick
out goods superior to what you yourself would
have an opportunity of choosing. You will generally find them carrying a small parcel, their
pockets stuffed with portable articles, and always a tolerable shabby great coat. An air of
deep interest, approaching the appearance of *care*,
seems imprinted on their countenances; arising
from the constant solicitude they entertain of
attracting the favour of every one they address,
and the seriousness necessary to impress upon
purchasers the goodness of their articles. Sometimes when they have offered one or two kinds of
goods, and are at a loss what you may be in want
of, they pretend to have jobbed away others
against them, in this manner: "only look at that
sample, my good Sir; turn it over; I never could
sell it so low, but having given cotton goods, by
which I got a good profit, in exchange, I can
afford to let these go at 20 per cent. under
cost price." Here a bill of the goods is produced
(nick named a " salt water invoice,") or a me-
morandum book, equally genuine, to prove his
words. Names of respectable persons who have
been his customers, are also adduced to raise your
confidence; and even the place of his own residence is mentioned, where a few years ago the

jobber lived in affluence. Such information is
seldom untrue; for they are for the most part
reduced tradesmen, (who have therefore a long
string of acquaintance,) that live by this mode of
carrying on trade: neither is the thing in itself
disreputable, unless when made so by the in-
troduction of arts and wiles, and misrepresenta-
tions to obtain sale, and cheatery in the weight or
measure when sold. It cannot be commendable,
either for the jobbers to watch strangers into
public houses, there to press upon them by plau-
sible arguments, articles for which they have no
immediate necessity; therefore, let me advise the
reader, with a

N. B. Not to make purchases in public houses
at all, even though he should once have known,
under very different circumstances, the poor man
who tenders his bargains for sale; for the practice of such an itinerant way of trade, with all
its concomitants of persuasion and deception,
effectuates an alteration in the character and
principles, as well as the manner of life, of the
best men in the world; while the balance in
point of numbers, is considerably in favour of the
totally different sort among us. For instance,
what ought we to think of a man, who, after
sustaining for years an unimpeachable name, and

filling a distinguished office in the city of London, should be found selling a pound of tea "plated?" that is, at top and bottom a thin layer of fine hyson, and in the middle the rankest bohea, of Dutch importation!

Next to these, as a warning to avoidance, we must notice the

BARKERS,

Who are of Moorfields origin, where they press you to buy household-goods and furniture; as they do clothes in Rosemary Lane, Seven Dials, Field Lane, and Houndsditch. Ladies dresses used to be *barked* pretty much in Cranbourn Alley and the neighbourhood of Leicester Square; but it is pleasant to have to notice the abatement of the nuisance in a great measure. The shop-women content themselves, now-a-days, with merely asking strangers to look at their goods.

I scarcely know what to recommend to my reader in such cases, for he would not like, perhaps, to follow my example: when these fellows were showing me from room to room, and dragging me upstairs and down, I used to manage to carry off portable articles, as ink-bottles—plated crewet-stands, small tea-caddies, and such like sort of little things as would easily squeeze

up and stow away. I may, however, repeat
what I have said elsewhere, and that is, " knock
down the man, or indeed the woman, who dares
to touch you with the hands :" should you wish
to decline this, at least huff the intruder with
" hands off, fellow !"

MOCK AUCTIONS.

Another set of these BARKERS are employed
at MOCK AUCTIONS, and no other. " Walk
in ! the auction is now on," or " just going to
begin," they utter, in coarse stentorian strains.
Such auctions are easily distinguished from the real
ones, notwithstanding they assume all the external marks of genuineness, even up to advertising
in the newspapers, and being held in the house of
a person lately gone away, or dead. They are
called mock auctions, because no intention exists
of selling under certain prices, previously fixed
upon ; which, although not high, is invariably too
much for the quality of the goods—which are
again of a very inferior cast. And, they are further known, by the anxiety evinced to show the
goods to strangers the moment they enter; by
the overstrained panegyrics bestowed upon every
thing put up ; by the exacerbated vocabulary of
the auctioneer, who endeavours to jest, to bully,

and to jaw you into a purchase, asking you in a
most petulant way, what you offer for this, that,
and the other ?   All night auctions are of this
sort : the seller having purchased the goods for
the express purpose of *auctioning them off*, often
pushing the price exorbitantly beyond the real
value ; asseverating that the manufacturer never
will be paid ; and increasing his earnestness the
more he lies, in order to keep up the delusion.

Sometimes, though the sale has not begun when
you enter, they will immediately begin business,
and perhaps one among them will pretend to
make a purchase ; not only so, he will even pay
down the money, so that this is likely to induce .
you to make a bidding.   An equally deep manœuvre is, the offer to take back, or exchange, the
articles under sale, for others in a day, a week, or
ten days.   This is more particularly the case with
watches : if you do so take them back, you pay
through the nose for the exchange, and you find
out too late you had better have taken Dr. Johnson's advice, and dealt " at a *stately* shop, at
once, where it would not be worth their while to
take you in for a pound or two, at the expence of
their reputation."

On the other hand, it is not to be denied, that
a great many bargains are met with at auctions

of even the worst sort; especially during the late few years of distressed trade, when manufacturers were in the habit of *raising the wind,* by sending goods to be sold for what they would fetch,—be that much or little. But here double destruction awaited them; the auctioneer proposes to give his acceptances at once for the sum total; or what is still worse, incites the deluded men to go on making more goods, to an immense amount; but before the bills become due, the acceptor decamps; the MART, (as such places are called) changes hands once or twice into the possession of his coadjutors, and after undergoing other transmogrifications, it is at length shut up.

This was precisely as it happened at the famous Mart outside Temple Bar, kept by little Williams. He "did the natives," as he used to term it, two or three times, transferring his *business* to one or other of. his colleagues. The last time was that in which he took in a poor hatter for a thousand silk hats, and another for twice the number of chip ones; a Yorkshire man for a great quantity of second broad cloths; another for kerseymeres, and pelisse cloths; and others for pipes of beer and of wine. The first description of hats, were sold at three shillings each less than cost price: the cloths in somewhat the same pro-

portions ; and the wine was bartered away to one
J——ºy, in Holborn, for linens ; but was afterwards recovered by action at law, when all those
facts came out.   One M——l made an abor-
tive effort to continue *the fun,* as F——r used to
call it ; but failed for want of that *gumption,* or
decidedly rogues' tricks, which is necessary in the
performance of *great* actions.

Upon this occasion, who can doubt, but that
great bargains were to be met with !   But then
the time it takes up, and the circumspection
necessary to avoid being taken in, besides the
chances that exist against the recurrence of the
same ingenious devices (little Williams being
dead) contribute to render an experiment unsafe.

IN PERAMBULATING THE STREETS

Either for business or for pleasure, the stranger
will have to withstand a great number of *subtle
contrivances* to come at his money, which we shall
treat upon in the last place ; meantime, we will
speak of those other more violent means, where
the *person* is *touched,* or his *mind* is *intimidated,*
to come at the same ends, viz. obtaining the property of the unwary stranger.

This is the most *philosophical* mode of arrange-
ment ; and as every thing is done now-a-days

by dint of head-work, we can discover no good reason why a little learning should not be introduced into the "London Guide." Certainly a plan much preferable to that gallimaufry of incoherencies, and antiquated rigmarole of precautions against evils that no longer exist,—of obsolete terms, and disused methods,—entitled "King's Frauds of London," scarcely a line in a page of which is applicable to the present times, and present practices; no more applicable to the present day, than the "Cheats of Scapin," or those of "Gil Blas," are to the present manners of Spain.

And yet the trash of that poor miserable *varment* has been adopted, and reprinted into Mr. Barrington's book, "The London Spy;" of which it comprises about one half, as near as I can reckon; another *quarter* of that *London Spy* is occupied either in telling us about horse-racing and other *country* cheats, or the details of mal-practices upon the river Thames, which no longer exist. These latter are copied out of one of the books I have by me, written twenty years ago, before those Docks were formed which entirely altered the practices. upon, and commercial appearance of *the river*. A man might as well talk of the beauties of Grecian building in the reign of king Harry, as of the

the frauds committed by "scuffle-hunters, mud-larks, light horsemen and heavy horsemen, upon the *trade* of the river Thames" that do not exist.*

The means of perpetrating these robberies are taken away, by the ships unloading in the docks, (three great basins, or more, enclosed with walls) into which it is impossible to penetrate improperly, and out of which no one goes without search, of whom there can be the *most distant doubt* as to accuracy of conduct. Aided by the active exertions of the marine-police, those extensive establishments have extinguished nearly all the old methods of robbing the ships and quays; in lieu of which, new and more daring acts of piracy have been adopted. Of these we shall speak hereafter; these observations being only used objectively, we shall here dismiss the subject for the present, to resume the course we just now pointed out—the exposure of such villains as extract your money by putting you in fear of personal injury.

If buffers and mock auctioneers intimidate by their vehement manner of pressing their wares upon you, no less do the KEEPERS OF STALLS

---

* Even the terms of art have changed: for instance the word cull or cully, a strumpet's kept man, then, now means a man taken in by her wiles.

impose upon the credulity of strangers, and treat them with incivility and even rudeness, when these decline to purchase their trumpery. " You did not want to *buy*," said one of these fellows to a well-dressed gentleman lately; " here have you pulled about my books, and asked the price of four or five, but don't know one that you want. No; you don't want to *buy*," said he with a sneer, insinuating that he was likely to steal!

At various points, ready made CLOTHES SHOPS employ Barkers at the door, who pace up and down before the window, and almost forcibly hand you into the shop; where you are set upon by two or three, who will get a garment upon you whether you are willing or no, demanding twice its real value, and if you are a *flat*, you cannot get out of it with the gentle use of *words*. Abuse follows you, if you *do not purchase ;* you are robbed if you *do*.

In what respect are such scum of tradesmen better than the well-defined villain, who being one of the

PILFERERS IN THE STREETS

runs off with the very garment you have bought.

If you carry the bundle yourself, one of these will run against you, or shuffle you along from

behind, and away goes your bundle or parcel.
His companion, if he has one, interrupts the pursuit, or joining it, impedes your progress, by
treading on your heels or kicking them up.

I have seen one of these shabby dogs (who
were always below my cut) take off a lady's tippet
in the street, at noon day ; nor has she discovered
it for the space of two minutes,—a time fully
sufficient for his purpose, and enough to ensure
his safety.   I thought this trick the nearest to
picking of pockets for neatness and cleverness, of
any I ever saw.   His plan was to loosen the tie
round the neck, by getting hold of the end of the
ribbon, and reaching over her shoulders point
out something in the window at which she stood
gaping, the bow was of course pulled through.
This manœuvre passed off very well ; for he held
in his hand the remains of an orange, and his accomplice occasioned an agitation among the
crowd at the same moment.   Lifting up the lower
corner of the tippet, another ribbon which fastened
it round the waist, was cut, and then gently
raising it near the back of the neck, he disengaged
it from all further obstacle—and *bolted*.   It was
a warm spring day, and I dare say she caught
no cold.

Others, still lower and more daring, knock off the hat, if it be a good one, and run away with it. The sufferer having received a pretty hard blow with hand or stick, is not in a condition immediately to follow ; and the pilferer, though a mean one, is safe enough from harm in a few seconds. Mr. Tufton was thus served in St. James's place (January, 15, 1818 ;) but the shabby perpetrator ran to a passage of the park which had then no outlet, and was taken accordingly.

Some again wait about the park, at the King's Mews, or wherever errand boys or porters set down their loads—the former to play, the latter to drink ; and while they are in the midst of their fun, away goes the goods committed to their care. A few go about who are *false* porters, or a kind of dog-sheep, who contrive to talk or toss up for gin, with the real ones, and meanwhile " ring the changes" by walking off with *their* loads. Upon opening the exchanged package, stones, or bricks, or (if a cask) vapid water, is found to inhabit a tolerably good looking external.

Not many years ago, a lot of young miscreants used to wait the coming out of day-scholars of an afternoon, at dusk ; and, affecting to be full of *lark*, make off with their hats, books, or great

coats. The prosecution of one of them, a Mulatto
boy of twenty, for an offence of this precise nature,
in Air Street, Piccadilly, put an end to the depredations of that gang; and the magistrate at
Marlborough Street in thanking our informant
for having secured the offender, assured the by-
standers, that no affected gloss of a sportive sort,
should guarantee to this nursery for thieves, impunity for their early offences. They begin with
small wares, and in time deal at wholesale.

Those who PROWL THE STREETS all day upon the
look-out, make a dead stand-still whenever people
are getting out of hackney, or stage coaches, to
see what may turn up to their profit. If a box, or
other package, is left a little astray, while the passenger is overjoyed at the meeting of his or her
friend, advantage is taken of the circumstance,
and it becomes fair game. It may so happen, if it
be a hackney coach, that the driver and the thief
may be acquainted; and then the former places
some of the luggage conveniently for carrying off,
as thus: standing rather wide, he puts the article
to be *boned* between his legs, and then reaching
into the coach for more, he steps forward a little,
so that his coat conceals from the view of his *fare*
both that part of the luggage and the thief;
the latter stooping down behind the hind-wheel

drags the article towards him, and bolts off.
Should the *fare* have gone into the house, the
same end is attained by planting the article to be
boned, a little on one side of the door, while honest Jarvy enters with another part of it. This
last is the cleverest way by half; but some people
by their vigilance prevent either the one or the
other from taking place. At any rate, those who
take hackney coaches with luggage (or indeed
without) should never permit the driver to take up
any one on the box, but peremptorily order such
fellows off; they two being invariably dishonest
palls: need it be added, that if he is thus driven
from the box, he gets up behind, or runs along-
side, the same hazard is incurred, of finding him
lurking about the coach at the end of your
ride!

The first-mentioned method of thieving, I have
seen practised upon fruit in Covent Garden market, at the earliest dawn of morning, when I have
been out upon my rambles. A coster-monger
demands the price of cherries, and makes a fair
bidding, which entitles him to look at the goods;
these, being packed in two-peck baskets, placed
one upon another, he removed the first between
his legs, while he reaches after another basket.
His confederate handed off the first, but the

L

seller prevented any more from being *disturbed,* or I make no doubt, from the activity of the second man, more would have gone the same way. The long fan-tail great coat of the first man, concealed the second from the view of the sufferer.

WAGGON DODGERS.

Fellows who follow after town carts, waggons, stage carts, and such like, to pick up any portable package that may remain unprotected for a moment; they are a needy sort of thieves, and partake a good deal of the character of the last-mentioned, to whom they assimilate in many respects. In my preregrinations forward and backward, I have seen a couple of them *dodge* a waggon from Picadilly to the city, in order to dislodge a poorish-looking box from its tail. With a wisp of straw in his hand, to conceal a knife, one of them cut the cords that fastened the box to the tail (to the *edge* of which he shoved it) ; he unbuckled the leather which crosses that hind part of the tilting ; and the motion which the faulty pavement now and then gave to the vehicle, soon shook about the straw and the box upon the ground. It would have been good prize, but for the interference of a *civilian,* who made himself busy with *the thing*, at the waggon-office in Friday Street.

These fag-ends of a low profession descend so very low, as to run off with a hare, that hangs-at the corner of the stage-delivery carts; cut off ropes at the ends of town-carts; attend at the markets to make prey of any packages of dead meat, flats of butter, or any other article that may come in their way, even to the very whips with which the butchers and green-grocers come to our markets. The curious part of our readers will be surprised to hear, that a poor fellow in Leadenhall market, and another at Newgate market, get a subsistance by taking care of the whips only, whilst the owners are in the market; for which he receives a precarious recompence. When meat or other articles are bargained for, and *booked* (as it is called), they must be taken away to the cart immediately, or left at the peril of the purchaser. Here again is a good scope for the dodgers: the buyer having been watched into a distant part of the market, away runs the rogue in great haste, calling out "here, you, Mr. Such-a-one's two fore-quarters of beef," and away he goes with one of them. In the winter of 1816-17, a cart-load of meat was driven from Ivy-lane and found in Type Street, Moorfields, and thereabouts was discharged of its contents.   The *Long alley* lads fed well that day ; and no doubt some part of the contents fetched *money*, as there is a butcher in the next alley, who has seen *foreign countries.*

Some of them wear an apron, or carry one in their hands, rolled up ; sometimes it is a bag— the better to cover smaller articles.   They turn their hands to any thing, in which they are occasionally assisted by their women.   Shopkeepers who expose their goods for sale at the doors are always open to their robberies.   The men practise it in this way : having marked out an article to be boned, they place their bag upon it, and go on to look at something else ; which, whilst they are replacing, with one hand, occasions no small trouble, and the exertions necessary to accomplish this, keeps the other hand at work in filling the bag—with which he walks off.   Books at stalls are fair game.

Their women go to linen-draper's shops, where the goods hang up at the door, and one standing behind the other, draws under the arm of the front one, whatever she may have fixed her mind upon: if it does not slide off readily, she cuts as much as she can reach.   For those sufferers there is very little commiseration : they expose their fascinating lure, and have no legitimate cause of complaint if they feel now and then a little nibbling at it. But for those who steal books, we do not say that they are fascinated with *learning*—they would *learn* better else; perhaps we shall be nearer the fact, when we attribute the fascination, mostly, to the money they may obtain for them at the *Fences.*

These fellows will join in a bullock-hunt, or purloin sheep from the drove—hold the clothes at a novice-fight, and run away with the *man's* covering; they will snatch off a woman's cloak—run off with a hat—lift up a sash for whatever may be within reach—or *mizzle* with umbrellas, that may be left to dry, or what not! If there is a riot on account of provisions, this class of people, women as well as men, are the most clamorous, although they never *buy* any; when the cheese and bacon dealers were *visited* so often, some twelve to sixteen years ago, these fellows stole the money in the shops at Clare market, Chiswell Street, and Cow-cross; but it is worthy of remark, that when one of them was recognised, he had the address to say, he took money to keep the people quiet outside, who threatened to pull the house down: no less so is it, that the sufferer put up with his loss *silently,* for fear of that very man! Is the criminal law of

this country well enforced, which should permit so
flagrant a dereliction to pass ? Too much is left
to individuals, to their kindness, pusillanimity or
soft-heartedness.

PROSTITUTES AND BEGGARS.

Their practices, as they are personal annoyances
in the streets, come next under consideration;
the former are most dangerous by day, (so completely is the avocation changed) the latter by
night. Both assume the character of robbers, as
suits their purpose.

By day, the number of women of the town, at
all points, equal those by night; and they are
more dangerous, because their blandishments, and
means of enticing the unwary, are set off most
floridly. The novice to their manners is easily
caught, as is frequently he who is versed in the
ways of town; for, to catch hold of the latter,
they will dress in the style of a neat servant-maid,
with perhaps a key of the front door, or a plate
in their hand, as if just stepping out upon an
errand. "What are you at, with that plate?"
said I, to an old one, whom I knew. "Catching
of *culls*," answered she. This was one Miss Ellis,
an Irish woman of very fine symmetry, who had
been in keeping in all the varied scenes of life,

from the top of the tree to the bottom. She was
thus strolling about, without bonnet, two miles
from home; *she*, upon whom the wind was not
permitted to blow, while under the protection of
Jack G———, exposed in this manner to the
dark air of an autumnal evening, reminds us of
the fallen greatness of Buonaparte, and the
abject state of Lord Chancellor Bacon's last years,
who was denied credit for a pint of porter,
as the ex-emperor was for his sincerest asseve-
rations.

In general, the *go is*, to put the best *toggery*
on that is to be had, adapted to the state of the
weather. For this purpose, if *the lady* has not
got clothes of her own, she can find them (on
hire) at the upper class of bad-houses; most of
which are extremely well furnished in that particular, deriving, from this source, no small part of
their profits. If she is a good *judge*, she will not
overdress herself, but trust for customers to her
eyes and limbs, both of which she manœuvres,
when she is *down* upon a *cull*, who becomes her
admirer. A good deal of ogling takes place on
her part; she pretends to modesty at first, perhaps, if her dress is corresponding thereto; but, if
she discovers her admirer knows a little too
much to take that in, she changes her tone to

an expected meeting, or an appointment with a
gentleman of consequence (a married man);
but the time of meeting being past she thinks
of walking homewards.

Such are the arts used to inveigle men, by the
force of their passions, into snares and trammels,
which last, some of them, to the end of their lives;
but if not, occasion disquietude, breach of rest,
and immediate distraction of the faculties, the
forerunners of deranged finances, a shallow purse,
and probably of ultimate want.

The Courtezan, whom we have supposed in-
veigling her inamorato to her lodgings, or a
brothel, having thus broadly hinted her wish to
return home, if he does not bite at that, proceeds
with the remainder of her *part*,—as the players
call it.   Probably she flatters his vanity, or self
love, calls him " charming fellow !"   Wishes he
would call a coach for her, see her into it, and
send her home; for she is " tired of waiting,
disgusted with the men," and heaves *a sigh*, to
think of their unfaithfulness.

Let us next suppose the coach approaches,
she presses him to accompany her home, but as
he cannot spare time, he need not stop a moment,
but only just see whereabout her dwelling is,
and he may come another time.   But should

he hesitate to order up the coach, she calls him
"shabby fellow ;" asks him if he imagined she
wanted him to pay ? and when she flounces into
it, gives her address distinctly, that he may know
where to find her, if his curiosity has been excited
by what has passed. Many of these high ones,
hand about cards of their address.

N. B. At whatever stage of the negociation,
his good resolutions give way to her arts, matters
not ; from that moment he is saddled with ex-
penses, and with inward reproaches, if not with
disease ; at least, so it happens in the majority of
cases. Whoever hearkens to the voice of the
Syren, is caught by her wiles. Tear yourselves
away, then, from its sound, ye yet uncontaminated young men, 'ere it be too late ; to hearken is
to be lost ;—to touch is to be undone.

One general proposal is made to every New-
comer, by these higher classes of Cyprians, which
is nothing less, than that he will take her into *keeping*. This is the rock upon which most persons of
warm dispositions split : if they once give ear to
her representations of its advantages and cheapness, of her love and attachment, he is ruined. It
does not signify to her, that she is already in keeping of one, two, or more ; she will *turn them up*
one after another, under the impression that she is

clever in selecting, or with a worse motive. The
purse waxes empty, or its strings become rigid
with use. Pleasures like these, (if indeed they
are so) pall upon the palate and vitiate by their
very odour. No delicacy, no sentiment, no soul,
takes part in the carousal ; and the indigestion,
the flatulencies of love, regurgitate upon the
palate, even to nauseousness.

Our readers, who are novices, will possibly be
surprised to hear, that many of those High-flyers,
though they keep, or job, a coach, and livery servants, can swear a good round stave as any fish-
fag at Billingsgate; some have more taste for that
than for prayers : how unlike ladies of the same
occupation in some foreign countries ! The
charming Miss Shaw, for instance, can say worse
things about her eyes, &c. (sparkle they never
so bright), than ever was said about the Duke of
M———h's *penchant* for her.

Many are the gradations from that highest
degree of prostitution, down to the trulls that
parade the streets by day ; and one or two more
steps, still, include those who keep out all night.
In the latter *dark* offenders the conduct is so
glaring, their robberies so soon unveil themselves,
and the men are so disgusted, that less personal
harm comes of them, than of those which *begin*

by day ; they are less likely to undergo repetition than these, and terminate in the night that gave them birth. Whereas the man who is open to woman's snares, while the mind is its own, is caught by the mind ; the very day-light adds a *gusto* to the illicitness of the amour, and its repetition is the consequence. The thousand numerous ills which follow, can scarcely be imagined ; for many a sad catastrophe never has come to light.

Possibly, the jealousy of two persons out of four is excited ; for, women of the town can be jealous of the wife of a man with whom they cohabit ; or, her former paramour may feel the same rankling passion, and avenge it by murder : or, perhaps, he may perpetrate the same horrid deed, with the connivance of their common mistress, when her cupidity has been excited by the display of much property on the victim's person. Now and then, we hear of a gentleman being lost, unaccountably : a few years since we knew of a learned gentleman being burnt, with the house, in Chandos Street, for which *accident* no other reasonable motive could be assigned, than the last mentioned one, since he had a great deal of money about him.

Not to quit our subject, we proceed to descant

on the dangers to be apprehended from the loose women by day ; and, by exposing their methods, put our readers upon their guard against such arts. Countrymen, in particular, and men of florid countenances, generally, are much sought after by old worn-out Harridans ; and, if they are low in life, sometimes get maintained until they become emaciated, and unfit for their lascivious purposes. The contaminated ossociation, bring such men into dishonest habits, and some of them suffer for their crimes. Such men should, above all things, avoid being well treated by old whores ; who upon first view might be mistaken for respectable housekeepers' wives : they are much worse to deal with than younger women, for this, among other reasons, that they know more roguery, and are remorseless in *spilling* the man whom they have, perhaps, themselves seduced to the commission of some offence.

The guilt of betraying her *Fancy* is not confined to the Harridan ; younger women of the town, are sometimes caught tripping in that way. In two years and a half, —————, (whose right name I never knew) lost three men in that awkward manner, one of whom was for a capital offence, so that she was *called upon,* to account for how it could have happened ? Whether

it was true that she alledged I know not, but
every body believed her, except the mother of
the young man who was *sentenced :* the truth is,
appearance and a good face do a great deal; for
I never did see a finer looking woman, from top
to toe, than she is; and when I saw her walking
down Fetter Lane, last Christmas, I could not
help comparing her to a ship under full sail.
The excuse she had to offer was, that " some of
the things [stolen] were found in her lodgings;
and the officers knew, without her impeaching,
how they came there." For the second man,
" that *they* watched her to where he lay concealed, and so found him out." No excuse was
offered for the third man; two out of three being
considered tolerably fair.

The reader ought to know, that her extrava-
gance, and importunities for money, drove the
first-mentioned man into his first and only
offence; thus giving to young men a severe and
thrilling lesson, of what they are to expect when
they attach themselves to women of the town,
be their figure and features never so fascinating.

Of a fine day, not less than twelve thousand
women of the town, of all degrees, except the
lowest, parade the streets in search of whom they
may devour. Neatness and cleanliness mark

M

them all: how much unlike the dirt of powder, and the frippery of thirty years ago! Indeed, health seems to prevail more and more among them: I say it, who am a pretty good judge of the matter.

From Aldgate Pump to Saint James's Street, is one universal line of march for them, broken at intervals by short turns upon the heel; and having, on the right and on the left, houses of resort; brothels, bawdy-houses and bagnios, which it would be ridiculous to particularise. Another line extends along Newgate Street, into Lincoln's Inn-fields, across Covent Garden, in various directions, through Cranbourn Alley,&c.into Picadilly. In those celebrated Alleys is the favorite shopping promenade of the BON TON; and here it is the greatest number of the high-flyers are to be met with, and the handsomest women; though the major part of them take one turn into the city, generally, every day, and back again. The third day-promenade for the fair Cyprians, is in Oxford Street, and the streets and squares leading out of it. Descending from the parishes of St. Ann's and Mary-le-bone, and out of all the streets on that side, they penetrate to Picadilly by Bond Street.

In this round of sensual blandishment the youth

of the metropolis have got to inhale their existence,
and with it the pestilential infection of example.
But they are inured to the sight from their earliest years, and some few of them go miraculous-
ly through the ordeal; the far greater part, however, plunge into the fiery furnace of debauchery,
and get seared in immoral ideas, and immoral
practices. These, repetition cannot harm, for the
seat of fine feelings is become callous. But, it is
the countryman or new comer, whom we would
exhort to guard against the pestilence, and the
snares, that every where await him, both without
and within. Internally, he feels the want of confidence in himself; externally he exhibits the
gait and habiliments of the novice, and is eyed
by the crafty, the wicked, and designing. He
must, then, at going forth, steel his mind against
the allurements that will be every where thrown
in his way; his eyes must be dim to the rain-
bow colours that scarcely cover, but do not
conceal, the alabaster forms that move beneath;
he must resolve to eschew the evil that will be offered to his ear; and to resist, with all his force,
the *tact* of pollution, that would endeavour to
excite the mere animal passions.

A practice used to prevail, for women to sit at
a window which had a good aspect, from which

they would throw out their allurements to the men as they passed,—beckoning them in. This has, however, been put down by order of the magistrates, on which account we should not have noticed it—our plan being rather to notice the evils that *be*, than those that *have been*—but as it may revive, and is very likely still to exist in a small degree, we think it part of our duty to warm incautious persons how they accept such invitations. Women so stationed are, for the most part, diseased, or under a course of medicine, which disables them from sallying forth;—the consequences of entering would be obvious and painful; and he who suffered death by such a step, deserves burying at a cross road, with the old English law inscription " FELO-DE-SE," placed over him.

It would be endless, and almost useless, but not at all entertaining, to enumerate all the means made use of to claim your attention by day :— by night, the address is more lascivious, but meant to be equally fascinating, being addressed to your grosser animal faculties and functions.

To call a coach for a lady, whoever or whatsoever she may be, is no great piece of service to perform by one of our sex for the other ; neither 'o hand her over the gutter, or across a street;

but when, in performing such an act of civility, you receive a squeeze of the hand, a thrust of the elbow, a leer, or a card of address,—learn that no good is intended : it is nothing more or less, than an attack on your purse; simply that, and not addressed to your person, this being a matter perfectly indifferent to her (whatever you yourself may think of its beauty.)—Her *flashman*, in her estimation, is ten times handsomer, certainly more acceptable. Where is the difference, then, of an attack on your purse, whether it be made by a man or a woman? through the medium of your passions, or of another's address and cunning?

We will, for a moment, suppose an unthinking young man led away by his passions, to give ear to one of those Syrens, and that she is of a decent stamp,—say a second rater, or a third, such as would not disgust at the first view :—What has he to expect upon accompanying her along? Her demand, at first but small, probably a few shillings, is enhanced by inuendo; as, how handsomely a gentleman (something like yourself) behaved last week, in a present of a few pounds. If you do not take this hint, she bothers you in the house of ill-fame, to which you may go; manages that you shall be charged extravagantly

for accommodation, and what you may drink,—
which, if you refuse to pay for, you get kicked
and abused by the bully, who is always in attendance, and understands the use of his fists.   The
same fellow contrives, too, to give you a good
character into the street, especially if you, have
taken your *cups,* so that you may be way-laid,
hustled, or tripped up, or knocked down, and
robbed.

You are under a mistake if you suppose be-
having handsome to *the girl,* will protect you
from this last act of violence; not always so,
but on the contrary, the display of your property,
or the exercise of your benevolence, proves you to
be *a flat,* and they take advantage accordingly of
your imbecility.   The best way is, to plead a
vacuity of purse, combined with the (pretended) wish to contribute hereafter more to her ease
and comfort, by a larger *douceur,* but that present circumstances prevent it.   *A large pro-*
mise goes farther than a *small performance,* with
such people.

At times, the importunities for relief from the
night-walkers, descend so low as a few pence, for
immediate sustenance, or rise to a glass of wine.
In case of the first, they take what you give;
and while laughing at your credulity, make far-

ther proffer of their persons, and increase their
demands with insinuated threats : in the second
case, you no sooner enter the tavern or gin-shop,
than several more of their companions surround
you, and the glass circulates to all round, including Flashmen, (thieves) with whom you are
thus obliged to associate, after having given way
to the first impulse. If you should escape with
pockets and person safe, after being thus encom-
passed by sin and wickedness, it would be strange
to me. That you would be put to much expence, is certain: that you would be robbed in
some way or other, little doubt exists in my
mind : that the effects of wine would render you
fitter for the workings of lasciviousness, is no
longer problematical. The fault lies, then, in
not resisting the first allurements : tear yourself
away, ere it be too late; lest, taking advantage of
hesitation, the seducer, versed in the arts of persuasion and lewdness, leads you an easy prey to
the shrine of her iniquities, and immolates you
upon the altar of her cold-hearted caresses.

But there are others, or rather some among
all those classes, who, not content with exposing
their blandishments, and giving invitations to the
brutish consummation of their wishes, lay violent
hands upon men passing along. Here again,

hesitation is ruin; irresolution will destroy you; want of decision is want of sense, and will soon prove the want of pence. **KNOCK THEM DOWN**, after having given them one notice to that effect; especially if it be late at night, or in a dark place adapted to robbery. Should you not adopt this advice instantly, your ideas of prudence will soon bend before your carnal appetites; and a couple of Cyprians will empty your pockets of their contents with the facility of a conjuror's wand. This advice may seem harsh to those who whine and cry out about " striking a weak woman." (Not so weak neither.) But I know what I am saying: when a woman ceases to behave like a woman, and assumes the character of the worst description of men, they are no longer women, but brutes. Shall a woman be allowed to exercise muscular powers, in aid of her lustful appetites,—to say nothing of meditated robbery—and then plead the weakness of her sex? The proposition is ridiculous, if not monstrous: a foot-pad robbery, then, is to be committed *with impunity*, because the perpetrator wears petticoats, and ——————— !

" Hands off!"—" Stand clear, there !"— " Get out, or I'll tip you a floorer!" These are the expressions, which, as they are under-

standable, or at least intelligible, to the meanest
capacities among them, are the likeliest to have
the desired effect; since they convey with them
an air of authority, and that *knowingness* upon
which I have so often insisted, when speaking
of other species of street-robberies.

Is my reader liable to get inebriated far from
his home? Let him take coach upon such occasions; or, if he call not a coach, let him make up
his mind to evade those harpies who ply at the
corners of avenues, streets, lanes, under the
piazzas, at shop doors, and such like. From these
dregs of an abject profession, what can be expected but filth, vermin, disease, and death?
Their breath is contamination, their touch is
infection, their views, in course, plunder, rapine—
and even murder follows. By such as these, men
have been decoyed away and totally lost, body
and goods; unless indeed the former might be
recognised at an anatomist's, or the latter at the
pawnbroker's. What other can be expected
of the fag-end of the worst finished part of vitia-
ted society, upon whom the pattern of their
maker is scarcely distinguishable? and whose
minds are embued with so small a portion of his
grace, that they appear a distinct race of beings

from those among whom they constantly dwell, and upon whom they hourly make prey.

Your charity is implored for the most abject looking beings that crawl the earth; and will you not bestow it? I answer NO! not at midnight; not when some latent purpose is in view; when the scowl that meets your eye, huddles together all the derelictions consequent upon an early initiation in vice and crime. Is there no means of reclamation? asks the abstract moralist: YES! it has been attempted upon a large and benevolent scale. Individuals, too, have exerted their individual beneficence; but the incorrigible wretches, with their adventitious cleanness, seek anew for fresh debaucheries, and spread wider and wider the impurities inseparable from an early initiation in "*the way of life,*" as it is called, quaintly enough. Notwithstanding this new *surface,* with which chance has covered their native garb of pollution, the original groundwork—the centrical alloy, still remains: no less vitiation of principle, nor less of pestilence exists, because, with a flimsy covering of new cotton, and the emblazoned whoredom of painted cheeks, the poison dazzles the eye, while the understanding is thrown into the shade. Look closer,

penetrate, and draw forth enough of ground-
work character, of which to make an analysis,
and you shall find the chief ingredients are the
same original base amalgama of iniquity as is first
above depicted. Men who are led astray by
such low-bred *vestals*, are not likely to possess
much discernment at the time, if they ever did
exceed their next-door *dolt ;* but they must be
far gone in liquor indeed, and in a such a state of
confirmed stupidity as to be scarcely worthy. of
being saved from the shipwreck, if they cannot
distinguish, when they get into the dirty purlieus
of St. Giles's, those of Orchard-street, Westminster, of Golden lane, or the Borough Clink ! If
they cannot see light from darkness, or the
difference between a cut-throat corner and a
dining room, they deserve neither commiseration
or help, in their misfortunes.

Low neighbourhoods like those which we have
named, have night-houses, where assemble the
worst and most unprincipled part of one sex,
waiting for prey to be brought in by the other.
Woe. to the man who ventures among them !
The unfledged youth, no more than the veteran
upon town, is their peculiar game; all is fish that
comes to net; old and young, gentle and simple,
when they once enter these pestiferous abodes, are

beset by half a score Urchins, who have been sitting
up, waiting for the return of the sisters (perhaps) of
one or more of them.   By a troop of both sexes
thus composed, and probably the unnatural pa-
rents themselves, is the dishonest pursuit kept up,
until their game has been robbed of every shilling
he has, together with his watch and miscellaneous
property, including his coat, hat, shoes, or other
clothes.   The unfortunate, silly man, is then to
be *mystified* (to borrow a French word) respecting the place he has visited; for which purpose
they throw themselves in his way, in order to
misdirect him; and this they contrive to do,
even although he should be too drunk, or too
sulky, too enquire, by means of a conversation
among themselves. The reflections and researches
of the next morning, teach him how weak an animal is man! How nearly resembling the brute
beast (when reason has departed at the approach
of ebriety), is that man, who dares to kill his
fellow animal, and ask for impunity, because it is
devoid of that reason, which he himself has bartered away for a few moments' gratification.

We must not deny that very many of those
girls have pretty faces, and appear as if just
escaped the trammels of a parent's care, or the
drudgery of a manufactory, and thus it is they

arouse the lecherous *gusto* of their paramours;
but, if mankind had nothing to resist, in con-
trouling their passions, there would be no virtue
in forbearing to gratify them.

Begging for liquor, is very common with every
class of out-door strumpets; frequently accompanied by the lewdest gesticulations, and offers
of their persons, in return; but, under circumstances the most favourable to a safe gratification
of the small pecuniary request, you would find
yourself egregiously deceived as to the amount
of the treat. They swallow incredible quantities
of liquid poison, under its various denominations;
and, if it be evening, demand something to eat,
something to be given to her "*sister*," (in iniquity) "a drop for that poor woman, and a glass
for this poor man, who was very kind to her when
the b—— officers wanted to take her away."
Such fellow being all the while her own Pal,
Flashman, or Fancy. And suppose the invitation
ends here? What have you done? I will tell,
though you dare not give it a thought: You
have encouraged the worst sort of mendicity;
You have associated with thieves and whores,
contributing your share towards fitting them
for further attacks; and you have run the
risque of losing yourself in that vortex, which has

N

swallowed up so many fine fellows before you. While thus treating them in a gin-shop, they will make free with your pocket handkerchief, or other more valuable article; sometimes when you do not order freely, one will pretend to square at you, and hit you in the pit of the stomach; and before you recover your wind, they get away safely—then you have leisure to search your pockets for what may be wanting.

Whatever is most subtle, whatever is most engaging in vice, has throughout been our chiefest, constant, wish to warn the novice against falling into. The coarser appeals to the mere man, his animal feelings and temperament, by the degraded set who ply the streets, have been already described; we come now to such as every man is likely to find at his lodgings, his place of business, or his resort for pleasure. As the last mentioned includes the theatre, as well as the tavern or public house, to which latter, at the season of agitated politics, almost every man of intelligence resorts occasionally,—we shall speak of it the first.

He who goes to the Theatres without some (large) portion of buoyancy of heart, is ill-fitted for the intellectual treat, or the moral lessons, furnished at them; but we will not suppose,

that he would go at all who was fitter for the
house of mourning, so the most we concede is,
that he may go with listlessness, out of politeness
to his companions. In either case he would
have to encounter that hot-bed of vice, *the lobby,*
in a state very unfit to undergo its scorching
ordeal. If he cannot withstand the temptation,
let'me conjure him to *act* with as much prudence
as the case will admit; above all things, let him
not *retire* and *come back again.* Let him not
treat two women at the same time, lest their ri-
vality should interest his *mind :* I say nothing
about the *heart* in these lucubrations, that is
quite out of the question; although I have
known a young man of character actually to
marry a girl of the town, who had paced all the
pavement in the *line of march,* and knew almost
every stone in its whole extent. What a pretty
brewing of mischief was in this false step? If
my reader must dally in *the lobby,* let him not
disclose his name, nor make a new appointment
with intention to keep it; let him turn a deaf
ear to one half that is said, and disbelieve the
other. Better than either would it be, to examine
the beauties that inhabit there, with the same apa-
thy that a florist examines his tulips, or the na-

turalist expands the wings of a butterfly, and transfixes its body against its last receptacle in his museum.

Observing these precautions, my reader will merely be done out of a little money, and probably a small portion of that laughing *hygeia* with which he entered London. He will then have conquered the most alluring species of destruction that environs our rougher sex; since here are collected all the most accomplished and fascinating outsides of the female form about town, together with the well-practised tongue, and every other art and blandishment to stir up and carry away captive the senses of youth.

At the tavern, there sits in the bar the fascinating lure of a pretty bar-maid, or a handsome landlady; sometimes both. Men in their *cups*, pass a word or two with these, and feel gratified; this ripens into longer conversations, an invitation to walk into that *sanctum sanctorum* of all groggishness follows, where the women as well as the men take their drops of *eye-water*. With one or the other (or both) of these, you are inveigled into an intimacy, an ogling, and then you are treated with

"Favours secret, sweet, and precious,"

as Burns rightly tells of Tam O'Shanter. Next
they go to the play-house, and you accompany
them; you squire them to Vauxhall, and your
business is done. You are either attached like an
heirloom to the house, become a sot, and make
room in half a year for a similar dupe; or else,
what is worse, you marry a ———, who has "tried
it on" with a dozen or two, and insists upon her
virtue being uncontaminated, because she has
never been but in company of gentlemen of
the house.

Every body must recollect the pother and run-
nings after there were in 1816, of a handsome
landlady, in Bacon Street, Spitalfields; and yet
she was not *handsome* either: her chief *forte* lay
in looking agreeable, and pleasing the foolish
part of our sex, without saying much, giving
each one to understand that he was the first in
her esteem. At least this was visible to us when
she lived in Cow-cross; and, it is to be presumed,
she carried the same guileful (though guiltless)
arts to her new house. We never went to the
latter, being already down to the hoax.

Servant maids in general (we might say uni-
versally) are upon the look-out for sweethearts,
and husbands; and indeed, this we may say of
the whole sex; but here we have nothing to do with

honourable or equal matches—it is of the fraudulent, or ill-begotten only, of which we shall here
speak.

Public-house attendants are most to be guard-
ed against; for they find you mellowed with
the fumes of liquor, to which they administer, by
the most scrupulous attention to your least wishes;
and having dressed for that purpose, throw out
their lures and fascinations, when the heart is
least capable of resistance. Most of them will
condescend to grant the *last favour*, if you are
base enough to talk about *marriage;* mention
the word *love*, and you may take almost any
personal liberties; for the mistress and master
enjoin her, as she values her situation, not to be
too *skittish* with good customers, nor too forward
with any; thus *judgmatically* dealing out that
which will "*do good to the house.*"

. These, as well as servant maidens in general,
(especially at lodging-houses) fix upon inexpe-
rienced young men, of whom the conquest seems
easy. Old harridans who are up to the *ways of
life*, after a dozen disappointments, dress out
lamb fashion, wear false curls, and paint a little,
nicely; subtract eight or ten years from their
age (nominally,) and thus entrap into marriage
boys of twenty, one or two, whose earnings or

little property, they hope to enjoy, together with his person;—as to *his* enjoying *her*, 'tis quite out of the question. *C'est toute autre chose.* This entrapping of young men, to marry elderly women, I consider to be as much a robbery (of personal happiness and daily income) as any act of violence committed upon the highway.

· N. B. Beware then, young men, of these latter description of women ! Eschew the tavern and public-house, if you cannot keep your eyes off the enticers there, go to bed and reflect; if you are pestered with the knowing old tabbies at home, and think what will be the feelings of your soul seven years hence to lie down with the ancient fair one, who now invites your caresses; for women of every degree make love, (I am ashamed to say) to the men in London. This accounts why, but is no apology for, the strange disclosures which daily take place here, of such out-of-the-way things as strangers would not think possible to happen, are coming to light;—of which murder is not the least frequent, incontinence the never failing attendant.

BEGGARS

May be divided into two species; the *bold* beggar and the *sneaking* beggar. The latter is self defined; being no other than those who abjectly implore your pity, and receive rebukes with meekness. Some among them, however, attempt *larceny*, and if discovered turn rusty upon your hands: of these we will speak hereafter.

The bold beggar is he who, with vociferations of his hard case, intimidates the chicken-hearted, the women and children; men of stronger mould also are sometimes choused out of their pence, and so far as the intimidation goes (with either the one or the other), it is no less a robbery than if a pistol was placed at your head, or a dagger at your throat. Half a dozen *sailor-dressed* men, for instance, will accost you in Blackfriars road, or Goswell Street, or Tottenham court road, or any other outlet, with " God bless your honour ! My noble Captain, drop a halfpenny in the hat for poor Jack; not a copper in the locker." On the ground is his hat, into which if you fail to drop a few pence, like Gil Blas in his history, you perceive what is most probably to be your fate, with this difference, that that Adven-

turer saw the end of a musket, you stand in awe
of a stumped arm. Those fellows sing frightfully,
and caper round you, ex-limbed, with as much
nimbleness as monkeys, showing by their leaps
the agility of squirrels or kangaroos, and leaving
you in doubt to which *order* they belong.   I am
firmly of opinion they are robbers, and nothing
else; as much so as he, who upon the highway,
tells you in good plain English "stop! and
deliver." What signifies the word or the gesticulations, so that the effect be the same on mind,
heart, and purse?

Another set of the bold-ones, are those who
knock at your doors, asking for charity, in loud
or very deep tones, in such a manner as to impress
you with the idea of preferring an immediate
donation of a few pence, to the fears of a protract-
ed interview, with such a character as that before
you. Should you refuse his request, he scarcely
deigns to make room for you to shut the door;
retiring the last leg most unwillingly, in the
strong hope that you may touch it, so as to ena-
ble him to cry out, or to swear *damnably*, or perhaps to knock again at the door, to demand sa-
tisfaction! Such as these, as well as the sailor-
looking men, first described, when you pass on
without relieving them, follow you a few yards

with imprecations on your proud aspect, call
you the most opprobrious name at the termination
of each sentence, and wish they had you in the
bilboes, on half allowance of water, &c. &c.

N. B. Upon first catching the eye of one of
these, put on a scowl, by drawing the eyebrows
close together; one shake of the head and "No,
not a stiver," finishes the business. If he press
the matter farther, and you vociferate "no" and
"never;" or some word inapplicable, in a strict
sense, to the terms of the demand, it will *bother
his whack*, and compel him to silence, from your
"superior knowledge of stuff and nonsense." For
example, he asks "your charity for God's sake,"
at each repetition you answer "can't, indeed!"
"Never!" "No; I didn't." "Not in all my
life!" "Could not think of it!" This mode is
not *taunting* the distresses of others : it is nothing
more or less, than *queering* the attempt of a *bold
beggar* to impose upon your softness. The really
distressed, claim a different sort of treatment, from
this sort of *queering*, as it is called

The *sneaking beggar*, who is not really and
unintentionally in distress, annoys you in the
streets, more particularly when you are in company of females, whose feelings he endeavours to
interest in his favour. His *whine* will follow

you half a mile, though his person is in the rear : latterly, however, the nimbler of foot, supplied with *religious* books, forces his wares upon your attention, which is first arrested on the olfactory nerve, and claiming, by a greasy effluvia, your subscription towards a replenishment of the nauseous offertory. Under other circumstances, they will creep into the premises of persons who carelessly leave open their fore doors, to pilfer whatever they can lay hands on. Gentlemens' kitchens, back doors, shops and warehouses they enter softly with imploring air : if discovered, they beg ; if not, they steal. A gentleman, of some spirit in *the city*, relates, that he was in the habit daily of reading the newspaper seated in the *dado* of his shop, while his people were getting ready to attend to their duty : he almost invariably found some of this species of rogues enter in the way we have described. He adds, that one day transacting business with a silk mercer, his neighbour, his face being towards the door, though at the whole distance of the warehouse, he saw enter one of those religious tract venders, who imagining he was unseen, shut up his book-shop and set off with a piece of silk : when overtaken and examined, he maintained stoutly that he was *employed* to carry it ; but upon being asked by whom ? he lifted up his eyes towards *the ceiling*, and made no further defence. He left his cause to " God and his country," and got off, as is too often done, by the connivance of his prosecutor, who made a wilful mistake in the indictment.

All descriptions of beggars sally out of town in the fine summer weather, some few take to harvesting, others to pilfering, and all beg their way back to town at the end of *the season*, in order to resume their old avocations and their former habits. Out of town, some will ask for alms at the front door while another gets over the walls behind.

One remark is worthy a place here ; and that is, the great number of beggars who are actually receiving parish relief, at the moment they are asking for eleemosynary help. Not the insufficient help which consists of a few shillings per week, to pay the rent of a wretched room, in which to rest their emaciated limbs, but meat, drink, washing, lodging, and clothes, sufficient for their subsistence. Impatience under restraint, however, and the love of a wandering life, propel many of them to seek, beyond the walls of a workhouse, the precarious alms of the generous and the undiscriminating part of the community.   A

few of them obtain *leave* to go out, in order, as is
said, to visit their friends; but the greater number
are *sent* out by the master of the house (who is
the contractor for their keep) that he may save
their rations for the day! This is most glaring, when he gives them threepence in money,
never more than fourpence each, with an assur-
ance that the walk will *do them good.* They are
expected to bring back broken victuals, or *something else,* for a regale at night.

Great annoyance is experienced, by many respectable people being applied to by beggars
with letters and petitions, which they buy ready
drawn up, and are couched in the most abject
terms; stating their sufferings, and exaggerating
their privations. They see your name upon the
door, and address a letter to you; if they find
out any of your acquaintance, they hesitate not to
name them, or put down their *signatures* to a
dirty list of subscriptions. They are mostly impostors, and deep ones, who adopt this scheme:
they must be resisted tooth and nail; for if you
relieve one you will have a shoal of his or her
cronies upon the same errand, at due intervals.
Pathetic addresses in the newspapers,—unless
well-authenticated, are to be suspected. Some

fellows, habited as clergyman, have been convicted of impositions with begging petitions.

HOUSE-BREAKERS

Abound most in dark winter nights; on which
account we seldom hear of the commission of
burglary in the line of streets where the newly in-
vented gas-lights are put up. This shows the
advantage of burning a light in your house all
night; the thieves drawing a conclusion from
that circumstance (unless they have previous confidential communication) that part of the family
are stirring.

Like all other forceful robbers, they are prone
to commit murder, if resisted; and it must be
in every one's recollection who reads, the " police
examinations," or attend to the disclosures of
the "Old Bailey Sessions" that they never go
unarmed,—mostly with fire arms.

We will not pretend to enumerate *all* the various methods of entering the premises of others,
which the law ever presumes to be " with intent
to steal." Was it possible this could be done,
and a complete exposition made of every manœuvre that has been tried up to the present day,
new, and yet unheard of, inventions would immediately be resorted to. Even on the day we

are writing, the last sad sentence of the law has
been carried into execution upon —— Attel, a
Shoreditch lad, who had found out a new method
of safely and securely robbing the next-door premises to his own for many months, and to a
ruinous amount for the poor sufferer. He removed a stair, both the *front* and *tread* of it,
in such a manner, as that each piece should slide
out of, and into its groove at pleasure. Through
this aperture he let himself down, and conveyed
away the goods when the family were asleep. His
detection was attended with the singular atrocity
of attempting uselessly to murder the victims of
his robberies; but in which he was foiled by the
more humane interposition of his accomplice!—
thus, no longer leaving to the mere invention of
fable, "The story of the two hired villains, the
one insatiate of blood, the other relenting, &c."
The children in the Wood, a tale and play.

There will be no reason, however, why we should
not describe those means which have been hitherto in use for house-breaking; that so, the yet
uninformed reader may know how to guard
against a repetition of the same, nor have to re-
proach himself for neglecting to take all the possible precautions for securing his house and premises against ordinary thieves.

Next to keeping a light burning all night, is
the affixing a large bell for an alarum on the *out-*
side of the house, having a communication with
two or more chambers.   This is more especially
essential out of town (or *around* town).   Your
next neighbours should be made acquainted with
its sound, possibly by *tolling* it at some given
hour; the same of watchmen, and patrols, horse
as well as foot; and the attention to the tones of
the latter would be wonderfully improved, if
the thing were to be done over a jug of ale. Having, in the next place, furnished yourself with a
good *strong* house-dog, and some *well kept* fire
arms, you may go to sleep in peace, provided
you know how to use the latter, and to manage
the former.   But servants are very likely to spoil
both the one and the other : the dog by too much
attention, the fire arms by too little.   What is
the object of firing off a charge of *powder* every
night at dusk ?   As soon as the dog is put upon
his station, this might be done, and it would be
a signal to him to be upon the " *qui vive ?* "
" Now mind, Cæsar ! Look out," say you, *and*
fire !

Whilst we are upon *precautions,* we may as
well make a finish of the general ones.

Should you at any time lose your dog, *mysteri-*

ously, by death or subtraction, do not go to bed that night or the next : something bad is intended ; possibly nothing less than breaking the dwelling-house ; more probably the robbing your out-houses, hen roosts, gardens, orchards, sheep folds, &c. &c.

If a servant leaves you *in dudgeon*, for some are very vindictive, or if one soon afterwards falls into bad habits, never suffer them to come near the premises, but look well to the *dog*, the state of the bell-pulls, and the condition of the fire arms. Should any thing be amiss with either of them, through negligence, suspect that some evil is designed ; should they appear to be deranged by design, be assured a robbery is in comtemplation.

The symptoms we have described, indicate that your domestics (one or the other of them) are leagued with thieves to break into the house. Then burn lights diligently, look to the dog, and the bell-pulls yourself ; and fire off your pistols, shotted, at some boarded place which will retain the shot to next day. This sort of league, or information from within, is called, " a put up robbery ;" although 'tis no less so, where mechanics or others have come at the secrets of "good booty, and the means of the easiest entry," to which they *put up* (as it is called) their palls, or else speak of those circumstances ill-advisedly. However the facts may come out, the effects are the same, whether negligently or criminally mentioned abroad, that much property is in a house that is ill-protected. The robbery at the Countess of Morton's, a few years ago, was owing to a very slight cause, like this we have alluded to.

False keys, and pick-locks, with the addition of a crow bar, are favourite modes of getting into houses, or of making their way through them when the entry is once made. Servant girls, who go of errands at evening, with their keys, should be careful not to leave such a dangerous instrument of robbery behind them; nor to suffer such to be purloined from off the counter of a shop, nor to be snatched from their fingers, in a sort of sport. She who should be thus served would find it but ill sport to be tied to the bed post half the night, whilst her former play fellows are handing off all the portable articles they can find. When one rogue had got possession of the key, another would watch her home; and the chief obstacle being thus removed from the front-door, the prey would be easy and certain,— as would the loss of her life be, were she to recognize any one among the thieves, *and say so.*

Young women should be most careful with what men they contract an acquaintance, for house-breakers frequently pretend love to servant girls, for the purpose of robbing the premises ; sometimes with the more shabby intention of robbing the girl herself of a *little* money, and a *little* clothes, together with all her virtue and peace of mind.

A house destined to be robbed, is first survey-ed by the parties ; for, it is too much to suppose half a dozen men would walk about with the proper *tools* in search of a job ! If an empty, or half finished house, be near,—or one is under repair,—whence the parapets, roofs or gutters are accessible to each other, this is chosen as the medium of communication ; and one of the party (or two) makes his way into that which is to be robbed, by way of the garret. Descending, ac-cording to circumstances, he seizes and binds, or gags, the only domestic (a female perhaps) who has care of the house. He lets in his com-panions at his leisure ; and they as leisurely bring carts if that be necessary, to strip the house, and carry away, even to the bare walls (we have seen it) as completely as if the king's tax-gatherer had *come in*, three quarters in arrear.

• Should the kitchen windows towards the area

be deemed the most vulnerable place, one of the
party descends, and breaks a pane of glass, which
enables him to push back the bolt, and he slides
up the window, the shutter whereof he forces
with a small crow-bar, and if the house be not
fully inhabited, he leisurely walks upstairs, and
admits his accomplices at the front door. In any
other case they go down the same way he has
done ; and in both cases it hashappened, that the
bold rogues have struck a light, drawn a cork or
two, and smoked their pipes, while stowing away
the valuables in a portable form ! Undoubtedly,
obstruction in any possible case, within the house,
would be attended with blood-shed ; but *before
getting in*, the tingling of a chamber bell, the
barking of a puppy, or the snoring of a servant
on the ground floor, would scare away the boldest
attempt that was ever made.

One of the most unblushing methods is, at once
to burst open the front door. A small *jack*, of
great powers, was known to have been used in
several cases, a few years ago. It has not been
heard of lately, and I am thence inclined to believe, there was but one of them made adapted to
this purpose. "With a purchase of one eighth
of an inch, you might heave St. Paul's with it,"
was a phrase used concerning the *Jack* ; and as

that purchase could be found at the interstices of
all pavements, it might be made the instrument
of a great deal of mischief.   Window shutters, as
well as doors, may be wrenched open, or burst
asunder by force ; but the noise this makes renders it too unsafe for the perpetrators, who do not
choose to "give a chance away," when any other
method remains to be tried.   Many men can
climb the front of a house as easily as others can
go up a pair of stairs : I have seen M———n,
the binder, *go it* in this manner, so as to astonish
even the *knowing ones ;* but as he is only an occasional thief, much evil cannot be expected from
his acquirements in this way, for some length of
time, at least, a parcel of cutlery, or a till-
box being his highest aim yet awhile.

Another plan is, with the old fashioned fastening of a pin through the shutter, to cut the wood-
work all round the head of the pin, by which means
the shutter opens, leaving the pin in its original
position.   This is effected by boring gimblet holes,
so as to admit the saw (made of watch spring) ;
and afterwards breaking a pane of glass so as to
come at the window fastening, then lifting it up,
the room in the first instance, and the whole
house ultimately, is at their disposal.

Seldom are these latter methods adopted that

the family, or some of the neighbourhood, are
not apprised of them at the moment of perpetration ; at the least, I have never gone into an enquiry on one of them, that persons have not been
awake to the business, more or less. Is it not
very strange, for instance, that an opposite neighbour's servant should discern a man traversing
from house to house, along the parapets, or the
roofs, at fall of the evening (or indeed any time
of the day) but apprise no one of it ? But such
is the fact with regard to several robberies in
Westminster and other parts of that end of town.
Again, eight or ten persons heard, or saw, the
sawing of the window shutter next to the watch-
house, in Newgate Street, (March, 1815),——even
the sufferer himself heard——but no one had the
presence of mind, or the activity, to interrupt
them; and " although twenty-two watchmen,
patrols, or constables passed within two yards of
the place while the business was in hand, yet the
thieves were not driven from their purpose, but
exchanged the time of the morning with the
watchmen," (See Times newspaper, and others of
March 4) one of whom was apparently upon
good terms with them. Whether he was so or
not, may be collected from the additional circumstance of his pulling down, repeatedly, the bills

that were affixed on the walls with a view to discover the thieves! Indeed, it must have been the
feeling, that the watchmen were near, which lul-
led the suspicions of those inhabitants into an
imaginary security.

Although it does not come within our province
to notice murders that are committed from
sudden gusts of passion, or the dark malignity
of offended pride, yet such as accompany
robbery are more certainly within our view.
As such we must notice a wide-spreading
calamity, in the perpetration of murder by
wholesale as the first step to burglary. Ever
since the murder of the family of Marr, in Rat-
cliffe Highway, and that immediately following,
of the Williamsons, in Gravel Lane, we have
heard of those compound atrocities more frequently than of any other species of *coal-black*
offence. The first mentioned was committed on
the master, mistress, and children of a haberdasher, who keeping his shop open until twelve
o'clock of a Saturday night, thereby allured the
murderer to take their lives, the easier to come at
the money, the receiving of which could not fail
to be seen from the street through the window.
A tolerably good lesson this for people who incautiously make a display of their property.

The second-named crime was committed on the bodies of a public house keeper, his wife and servant, by one of their guests, who had concealed himself in the cellar. When the deceased came to close up finally his bar, and to lock away the money, it is concluded the villain made his appearance, and perpetrated his diabolical purpose. A small degree of circumspection might have prevented this, and indeed the whole catalogue of crimes of the *deepest* atrocity; whereas, the lesser ones, people in general, take the most precautions to secure themselves from being made the tools of, mis-judgingly concluding, that those of blackest hue, are never to fall to their share.

How unreflecting are the robbers as well as the robbed, occasionally! When Mr. Wilkinson's premises in Moorfields were broken into about Christmas, 1816, and nearly one hundred and fifty pounds stolen, the gang were so incautious as to regale themselves next night, at the Punch bowl, Long alley, not one hundred yards off; where they were *nosed* by an old woman, whose teeth they knocked out, but were themselves taken in consequence. At the same house, just a year after, two officers called out a thief, to give him the information "that he lay under *suspicion*, and they

meant he should go along with them." No
sooner was he *up* to their message, than a shrill
whistle raised the attention of his companions in
the skittle ground: they were *down as a nail* in
five seconds, and the whole party of thirty or
forty *interfered* to prevent the *consequences;*
and although "the man was got away," yet the
officers—now three in number, were dreadfully
misused, one of them almost *massacreed*, and all
of them were " spoiled for plum pudding eating"
during the holidays which followed, and which
they gave to their stomachs—appetite having
taken ". leave of absence."

The first mentioned was the lot attached to
Jack Pettit, whose girl and two companions had
the lag for *fourteen ;* the latter case hath yet to
undergo investigation, before that awful court
whose painful task is to pronounce the harshest
sentences of the law.—We therefore forbear to
say more at present, for obvious reasons.

" The proof of the pudding is. in the eating,"
says an old saw, (and *old saws* are good sometimes). We are this moment informed of the
attack and defence of a [lone] house by three
women against as many men, at the least, which
story goes to establish what is said a few pages
higher up of the security to be reposed in,

when your house is protected by lights, a dog, and fire-arms; and goes to prove also the decisive victory which would have attended one other precaution which we recommended—viz. a bell, hung on the outside of the house — but which was here wanting.

Mr. W——— having occasion to leave home, for some days, the house was left under the protection of his lady and two maid servants: this circumstance was known; and an hour after dark the house was beset by two or three men, who were suspected of no good intentions, so the doors were well fastened by the female inhabitants. The lights were kept in, and all three kept strict watch; so that the first attack did not take place until eleven o'clock, which was commenced with fruitless endeavours to enter by the front door. Mrs. W——— here shewed that heroism, which sometimes, though seldom, discovers itself in the female character, upon great or paramount occasions. She flew to the door, which they were at that moment forcing with a crow, as is supposed; from the inside she harangued them, with promises of a warm reception for the first that should enter; and ordered down the blunderbuss, &c. for that purpose. "I shall not prevent your *coming in*," said she, "but be

assured I shall take good care that one or two of
you shall not *go out* again alive." The house
dog seconded its mistress, with all its sagacity,
and seemed to say with her, " come along scoundrels ;" while the two affrighted servants did all
in their power to infuse that fear, which alone
belongs to the base born, and the guilty. They
now abandoned the attack on the door.

A very few minutes elapsed when the dog
showed symptoms of the enemy being again at
work ; they had piled up loose bricks which lay
about, and ascended to the top of the parlour
window. This point Mrs. W—— thought they
would penetrate, for they were visible from the
upper part, or aperture ; she therefore took her
station at a distant part of the room, that the shot
might spread, so as to hit the whole of the party
that might present themselves on the shutter
giving way, which was every moment expected.
She called to them again, let go the spring
sword of the blunderbuss, and hitting the window
with it, gave them the same assurances, as before;
then retreated, and took a glass of wine ! within
their view, as is apprehended. This was too much
for their stomachs, and they retreated for the present.

Hours elapsed before a third endeavour was

made to get in by the cellar door; in which they
so nearly succeeded, that the arm of one was
visible from within; but the besieged being on
the alert, the villain retired his arm in great haste,
to avoid the thrust to which it was thus exposed,
and the effects of which he did but just escape.
At four o'clock in the morning, the assailants
drew off; but their retreat would have been *cut
off* by the timely use of a bell, at any moment
of their endeavours to break in.

"A word to the wise is enough," or ought to
be so; this descriptive narrative speaking more
than volumes can, to persons who are open to
practical advice; let the morose and the self-
sufficient suffer, if they neglect it.

A very common practice is, to break a pane of
glass near the window-fastening, which can be
soon displaced by introducing the hand at the
aperture thus made. Shop windows are frequently entered by the same means; but the breaking
is generally effected with a glazier's diamond:
as the shopmen are near at hand and might hear
the glass fall, a *sucker** is employed and placed
on the pannel in the first instance; then having

---

* The sucker is a small piece of tanned leather, which
being well soaked in chamber lies, with a string in the
centre, will thus heave a weight of ten or fifteen pounds.

cut all round near the frame, the piece is hawled out, and a good booty no longer remains problematical. Phosphorus, in a narrow necked bottle, after being ignited is traced in .the line the diamond is meant to take, which renders the glass soft enough for even a common knife to cut out, without making a noise.

N. B. In examining your premises to *see* whether your doors and shutters are safe, it is proper to *feel* also; for the house-breakers furnish themselves with coloured papers, near to that of the wood work attacked, with which they cover over an aperture until they can return to finish the job. Like street robbers, these fellows have whistles, and calls, sometimes a word, as " go along, Bob," that is to say,—" proceed vigorously in the robbery ;" again, " it won't do," is the signal for desisting, &c.

After all the precautions that are used to keep out the thieves from your house, they prove lamentably ineffectual from the superior cunning or prowess with which their calling endows them. First having found out some of your connexions, they come and induce you to put aside that excellent preventive of sudden intrusion at night—a chain on the door. This is dexterously done by means of a letter, and the bold

assumption of a friend's name, from whom they
pretend to come.   Once inside, all goes to wreck.
—Doors, locks, bolts, boxes and safes—even the
lives of the inmates, be they more or less, are
sacrificed to their vengeance, or their ideas of securing impunity.   The murders and robbery of
Mr. Bird and his housekeeper at Greenwich,
lately, was of this description; and we see how
difficult of discovery is the perpetration of the
compound villainy, that thus sweeps all before
its remorseless fangs.   Charles H——y, a footman
out of place it seems, residing opposite that
ill-fated pair, marked them out for his victims.

N. B. When any point is suspected of being
vulnerable, or that attempts have been made
there, the approach of the villains may be better
ascertained by strewing a few coal ashes near the
spot, if the ground be not too soft: although
they should come without shoes, the crushing is
sure to be heard.

SHOP-LIFTING

Defines itself.   It is the act of lifting up, in order to carry away, slily, goods from a shop or
warehouse; and is carried on to a great extent.
We spoke of those who steal *from the doors* of
shops, the goods *exposed* at them to invite custo-

mers, under the head of street robberies. In
the next place, the same class, and some
carrying their heads much higher in life, enter a
a shop which is pretty well beset by customers,
some of whom no doubt are of their own stamp
and connexions. Those women who are adepts,
wear the round-about pockets, of very large di-
·mensions, of which we before spoke under the
head of " Prostitutes." These generally go in
couples, sometimes more, the better to engage
the attention of the shopman, whose attention,
being fully occupied in present business, cannot
by possibility be paid in two places at the same
time. Suppose, as is often the case, ten or dozen pieces of printed cotton lie upon the counter
all of a heap ; they form a pile nearly as high as
your nose, or are shoved together by the thief,
the better to form a barrier against the sight of
the shopman. Muslin being the favorite object of
pursuit, a piece of it is buried underneath the
printed goods, or some of its own quality, and
she who is to take it, withdraws it quickly, as
soon as the *item* is given and perceived. If it be
a whole piece, the quantity would be too much for
any other than a bulky woman : her size would
carry off as much as thirty or forty yards without
creating much suspicion, though their eagerness

is such that the very thinnest would *try it on*
with the most bulky article.

The skirt or upper petticoat *is* made with a
very large pocket hole, or slit half way down;
into this the bulky woman thrusts the end of the
muslin (or other cloth, when that is not come-at-
able) then slides her *round about* pocket over it,
like a case; and after pushing her sides alternate-
ly against the counter, or against her accomplice,
so as to bend it under the projecting belly, off
she marches, under the pretence of going to some
other tradesman in order to save time. " Vell, I
declares! how long you are a choosing, Mrs.
Vatkins! I can't stop no longer here, but vill go
to Mr. Proones's over the vay for my tea and my
sugar. You come." Outside is another " to
take it away," lest there should be an outcry.
This is done in a court or narrow passage, but
more frequently at the gin-shop; the keepers of
which are sometimes made the holders of stolen
goods, without knowing it, thinking, to be sure,
that they thereby oblige a customer who is to call
again. What can amend this facility to the
escape of the guilty, but compelling the publican
to place the article where it might be open to
the view of every one coming in?

Although we have given this insight of shop-lifting in its most bulky form, it is not to be supposed that the ladies confine their speculations and practices to muslin alone, nor to the poor linen draper's shops exclusively. Haberdasher's shops contain equal fascinations for the leading foible of the female mind, unchastened in the school of philosophy—dress! All-powerful dress, and the over adornment of nature's fairest work, leads even *ladies* to commit crimes which their own sempstresses would shudder to contemplate. Ladies of the highest surface-character have been known to rob shops repeatedly, and require the vigilance of the warehousemen as much as women in the humbler walks of life. Without ripping open old sores, or abrading the film which covers the wounded character of a certain fair one, we must be content with merely making the assertion, and asking credit for it from our readers. As this is almost the only instance in which we have shown any disposition to *mealy mouthedness,* we demand excuse.

Lace was the object of solicitude in the case just alluded to; and is the favourite article of purloinment with those who follow shop-lifting as a profession : the largest value being contained in the smallest space, admirably fits this article to claim the preference.

The large hairy muff is charmingly adapted to facilitate this species of robbery : it being placed upon one arm, and the attention of the shopman directed to some article contained in a drawer or shelf she is sure is situated just behind, enables the lady to pick up with perfect impunity whatever she chooses, whether that be lace, ribbons, gloves, trinkets, books, or other desirable article.

The *ridicule*, which in summer supplies the place of the muff, sometimes raises suspicion from its capaciousness, and is no less adapted to receive the hasty acquisitions of its owner. Shopmen would do well to make an end of their bargaining and fancying, respecting one article, before they take down another ; with the additional precaution of counting the number of pieces, pairs, &c. of each, that he may place before his customer. This would *prevent* a great proportion of those shop robberies, which the tradesman *feels* has been committed, without knowing upon whom to fix the crime, and half distracted at his own suspicions, he robs himself of peace and the people around him of their comfort : and, as prevention shall be better than cure (all to nothing) any time of the day, " such shopmen are guilty (the law ought to say) who are so far derelict in their duty as to hold out the lure to their master's cus-

tomers—of much confusion in his goods and
negligence in shewing them."

If small articles are liable to be thus purloined, no less so are the most ponderous; only
these do not occur so often possibly as the former.   What will the unknowing reader think of
a man running away with a smith's anvil of
three hundred weight ?   He may stare! but it is
not a whit the more untrue, because he happens
never to have heard of such a thing.   I saw
it myself, in open day, not in a remote corner
of the town, but at the corner of Greek Street
and King Street, Soho.   The owners names were
Jackson and Bartlett; and the anvil stood just
inside the door, either to show that they were
ironmongers, or to perform odd jobs upon.   The
facetiousness of the last named gentleman induced him to follow, and compel the thief to *walk
back* with his load! assuring him, ironically, that
he was going the *wrong way,* and promising him
something for the extra trouble he was giving to
him; and he performed his promise : it was no
other than a jolly good kick in the —— which
he had for his pains.

What is it to me, or to you, reader! that this
happened long ago ? Have you not got *names* for
the fact ? and the date is a dozen years back at

of age, who *went* by no other name than " the
tall-one." He always had one or two books
upon him (as Paddy Byrne used to phrase it,)
and I really think he was religious in the main;
for he- never swore at all, nor was he *flash* to
slang, however ordinary. There is a north country saying, that " the silent sow sucks up the
most broth; so this *tall-one*, who had but little to
say upon any subject, and nothing upon several,
had a happy knack of disposing of his books, so
as to make them tell double and treble. It was
thus: going into a bookseller's to sell what he
might have, he chaffered a good deal about price;
and during the interest this would excite in the
mind of the buyer, he endeavoured to pocket
some other books. Should this not be possible,
in consequence of superior vigilance, or of the
undivided attention of the people of the shop,
he would make some excuse to leave his book,
and calling again when the first person was out
of the way, or at dinner, would reclaim his book,
but send it up stairs, &c. the better for the person to assure himself that the application was all
correct and *honest*.· This manœuvre enabled
him to pick and cull, or to pocket any article he
might have fixed upon. I have known him to
sell an article by description, before he stole it.

I call that *clever ;* as it is also to live a month
genteelly upon an original stock of only four or
five prayer-books, with which he rung the changes,
at the booksellers : giving those and *taking*
books, and *receiving* money in return. But
he *put his foot in it,* by overdoing his good
luck, as most people do, who know not what
it is to rule and govern themselves. He *took*
three volumes of Spectator, to sell by way of
sampler the remainder of the set, which he stated
to be ten, but the bookseller insisted was complete only in forty-five volumes. He at length
agreed for the whole forty-five, which he *meant* to
steal, as he proposed to bring them by piecemeal ; but Mr. Gosling of Castle Street, Leicester
fields (the right owner) would not let them go
in that way, and candidly told him so. The
holder of the three volumes, too, supected him ;
and both these having mentioned their suspicions
at a third bookseller's—the tall-one's schemes
were blown up, and the books returned to their
fellows in the set.

Than the shop-lifter's, there is not a more im-
provident set of thieves in the whole list. Not
content with one or two good things of a day,
they will go on from shop to shop, throughout the
whole blessed day ; so that they get watched by

the officers, who know them, from that circumstance, and from walking singly, one after another,
occasionally stopping, overtaking, and talking together with apparently great interest : then they
divide, and enter the shop just agreed upon, by
one or two at a time, as before described. If the
shopkeepers were to adopt the precaution we gave
a little higher up, they would be able to know
in a minute or two what they had lost ; and thus
contribute to the instant detection of the offenders, by immediately informing the officers what
goods had been stolen ; for these active men run
into the shops as soon as the thieves leave them,
to enquire what has been missed ? A question
which the shopmen seldom answer in the affirmative,—for the stupids really do not know ; more
shame for them !

In the same way it is the officers find out the

SMASHERS*

Or passers of bad money ; many of whom are
identically the same as the shop-lifters. But the
difference in the keenness of the pursuit is most
apparent: the reward upon conviction of the
latter description being more liberal and more

---

* See pages 2 and 12.

certain; and two or three officers find it worth
their while to spend a whole day in thus pursuing
them from shop to shop, until they are discovered,
—one or the other always keeping them in view,
when another is making his hasty enquiries, as
above mentioned.

Under this head we must class the passers of *bad
notes,* or forgeries of the Bank of England *cash
notes;* nor do we see why the *ruses* which rogues
have recourse to, the better to get rid of *stolen
notes* (or those which are otherwise improperly
come by) should not be considered of the same
genus : all three involve their utterers in the
same penalty—death ; and all require the same
management to avoid detection, or even pursuit.
For instance, a man received a ten pound note
too much for a cheque on a bank (Masterman's)
—he affects that he has not received more than
the right sum, for aught he knew ; or, if he has,
that he paid it away again just as he received it.
Upon coming *to trial,* however, it turns out that he
goes to a shop in Red Lion Street, Holborn, from
which it is sent to the public-house to be changed ;
and up to this latter place it is traced from the
Bank of England. Proving, in this manner, the
fellow as dishonest as if he had come at the property by means of burglary or of highway rob-

Q 3

bery. Hence upwards there ascend gradations
of guilt, as variously featured as the actors in
them are numerous; but is it not a little extra-
ordinary that the *makers* of forged notes are never
found out ?   The engraver ! the paper-maker !
the rolling press ! all are buried in the obscurity
of night, and bid fair to leave old Patch-Price,
the single instance of a combination of the triple
talent in one man.   Forty-seven prosecutions a-
year, upon an average of twelve years, are
brought by the Bank against the tools and
agents of the forgers, but not one in thirty years
against the principals.   How ! and why is this?

Not one of these forgeries ever met my eye,
that I was not convinced I could have discovered
of my own accord ; but although there were
any positively bad in my hands or those of my
friends, I have the means of passing them safely,
in such a way, that the Bank never prosecute, for
they never discover them from their own.

How few give their right name and residence
on changing notes at the Bank !

MULTITUDES OF MINOR CHEATS

Infest the doors of decent people of every degree
in society, and some of them press forward even
to your study, and infringe upon your retirement.

PRETENDERS TO LITERATURE,

And pretenders to superior sanctity, (teachers,) are the worst characters of this class, for they know just enough to feel that they are impostors, in their degree. French emigrants, partaking of both descriptions, a few years ago, overran the land; the *queue* of that safety-seeking race still inhabit here, and teach their doubtful morals, and a deference for their language it by no means deserves. The nobility and gentry were the chief dupes of those fawning hypocrites; but they descended also into the kitchen, and tasted in the pantries of middling tradesmen the good cheer of John Bull; while they despised his manners, and honest blunt prejudices, which has kept his more genuine offspring uncontaminated with the monkey-tricks and false philosophy which was imported with their fears. The consequences are, that our manners have undergone a change by no means for the better, (which they ought to have done when altered at all) and our language is contaminated to the last degree of *Frenchification.* At the tables of those who can afford to give them good dinners, we find those of our own (triple) nation in abundance, who pretend to an intimate acquaintance with

modern, if not ancient, literature ; but who are
certainly impostors in just the same degree as
they assume more than they know.

All those pretenders cheat you out of every
mouthful you permit them to devour ; out of
every shilling you may advance them by way of
loan, or as payment for you own or your childrens'
improvement, (if the becoming mere *jargonists*
be improvement.)   There is too much of *argu-
ment* in all our conversations, male and female,
now-a-days, in consequence; and those were
the sources of the hateful use of question
and answer in the commonest occurrences of
life.

PRETENDED CLERGYMEN.

Fellows who, without any previous preparation,
or even the laying on of hands (so much vaunted)
contrive to ingratiate themselves into the good
graces of the daughters, wives, and widows of
our more wealthy citizens, who would fain persuade you (as they have persuaded themselves)
that their mission is from *above*, whereas nothing
is better known, than that some few of them had
pretty extensive dealings *below.*   Every one
must have heard of the *Reverend* John Church!
Here I hope the *truly pious* clergyman will for-

give me for using the word ironically ; for there never could at any moment be a particle of real reverence borne towards a preacher, who laying under imputations of a heinous nature, should acknowledge them in the pulpit. His congregation seemed even to stick to him the closer, the more proof of his guilt there was adduced against him ; until at length the inexorable *fiat* of the law took him from their sight into solitary imprisonment.

Who has not heard of O'Meara, who by dint of corruption, and a harlot's interest, sought to seat himself in one of the highest pinnacles of the church ? Mrs. Clarke had another of the same *cloth,* who intermeddled in her dirty business ; and the *Reverend* Mr. Williams, was only discharged from the custody of the sergeant at arms upon a plea of madness. Not so mad, either : he can play a rubber at whist, or a game at cribbage, as keenly as the best that ever lived ; and although he seems lame, if he loses he can run away ; if he wins he can threaten, hector, bully, and, it is believed, can fight. He can *swear* too ; but once on a time the magistrate would not permit him.

The reverend Augustus B***y is no longer a clergyman, though he has undergone his degrees, and has advanced a step or two in the church : he is perpetual president of the butcher-meeting at the corner of Newgate Market. Another of the *ir-reverends* is a dabster at back-gammon, attached to ale, loves a good dinner, talks *jolly,* sings a (bad) song ; and has been found upon *the lay,* for which he caught *quod.* He gambles deep and long, and is always down upon the countryman : I know not to what *kidney* he belongs ; but hear, he has tried *three sorts of belief* or of discipline, from which I conclude he must be a Trinitarian. I shall not tell his name outright, for two reasons : 1. because he has *stood the patter;* 2. because he was always civil, and once very kind to me when I was *misused,* like him : it very much resembles *a brisk wind blowing in the dark.*

Great numbers of such as we have described pervade town ; but our readers must not permit their reverence for the cloth, to sway their judgment into the slightest deference for the men.

About twenty years ago, (and less by eight or ten,) there was a kind of house of call for journey-men parsons, who met at the King's Head near St. Paul's every Saturday. There you might see the Reverend Mr. Jones, and the Reverend Mr. Styles settling a change of service for to-morrow : a dispute between Dr. D——n and Denis Lawler, the playwright; scraps of Latin thrown out to bother the Reverend Mr. M——y, and to remind him of Inverness·and Gibraltar,—together with a dozen other incongruities.

If those clergy, as they are improperly called, familiarize with your families, and under the garb of sanctity, obtain the ear and the —— of its females (all for pure christian love.) There are

PRETENDED DOCTORS,

Who are no less dangerous, if admitted into your friendship or that of the female part of your family. One of these, named ————, was lately discovered debauching the wife of his benefactor under circumstances of the most aggravating nature. Many of them pay attention to the pecuniary concerns of your families, whilst pretending to administer to their corporeal evils: such fellows contrive to become executors to the wills of their dying patients, or to marry the daughters of such as are tolerably rich; and then they become (what is called) "regular;" though their previous, education, in most cases, only qualify them for serving in a haberdasher's or a draper's shop, or probably the still more honourable employment of shaving and hair-cut-

ting.   We now know persons who have emerged
out of those *professions*, and become *regular;*
but can the lion change its skin or the leopard
its spots ?

Nostrum-mongers abound, who prepare some
panacea, that will cure various and discordant
disorders ; thus playing with the lives perhaps,
certainly with the health and happiness of those
who hearken to their advice.

Hand-bills and advertisements are the chiefest
means of obtaining notice, the details of which
are too disgusting to be copied into these pages.
Whoever have been unfortunate enough to contract a certain loathsome disease, should be upon
their guard against pretended doctors, whose
chief object is to keep them in hand a long time,
in order to make more charges : the fellows who
sell ready-made medicines (called *patent*) are
arrant cheats, inasmuch as the same preparation
cannot effect a cure in two stages of the same
disorder.   The publican's paper (as it is called)
is almost daily crowded with these filthy invitations, and bombastic pretentions. Ladies, persons
of delicacy, the totally uninformed on libidinous
subjects, have that undescirable propensity thus
continually pressed upon their notice, by being
put immediately into their hands.   This part of

our complaint has abated considerably of late;
and ought to be put down altogether.

PRETENDED LAWYERS,

or those who propose to transact your affairs by
way of agency, calling themselves "Law Agents;"
and "Accomptants" partake somewhat of the
character of the Sycophants or useful men
whom we described higher up. These gentry
are mostly clerks of pettifogging lawyers, who
permit them to sue in their names for debts,
real or imaginary, actions for damages, assaults,
&c. They are at times such as *have been* in good
clerkships, but now out of employment; and
they constantly talk of the respectable concerns
to which they once belonged: "this was
always the practice at B. and A.'s, when I was
there;" "*We* never failed to get the money by
these means," says the pettifogger, in order to
give his advice an air of consequence. A great
proportion of them know no more of law than what
they have learnt "Over the water," or at "No.
9, Fleet Market."* These are admirably fitted
for "Agents" in the Debtors Court, under the

* The King's Bench and Fleet Prisons are thus quaintly
described.

R.

Insolvent Act; but their charges are generally double or treble those of the more respectable
regular practitioner. A few, however, have been
actual practitioners; but some aberrations of
conduct having offended "the Court," it has
struck them off its rolls. They generally *practise*
about the police-offices, and at the Old Bailey,
"for the defence;" that is to say, for the prisoners;
in which way they become the acquaintance and
familiars of the blackest rogues and thieves in
or about town. The history of one will serve for
that of all; though we must premise, there are
two persons of the same initial letter, which is
all we shall say for distinctions' sake. Our
hasty sketch of Mr. B. commences fifteen or sixteen years ago, when we find him standing in
the pillory, at Blandford in Dorsetshire, for *threatening* to inform against a glover, on the stamp
duty, and demanding money to forego the action!
Then it was he was struck off, with some severe
notice of the chief justice; and ever since he
has lived by his wits, as an informer generally,
but we have reason to believe we have seen him
on the lay also; at least he has been present
when *things* have been *done*. In summer time
he visited Margate, Brighton, and other fashionable
resorts, laying the gambling-tables under contri-

bution, and threatening informations against illegal games of chance, then very prevalent; receiving in return for his trouble, and to purchase his silence, sums proportioned to business done;—this profitable trade continued as long as the evil lasted. . Until Silver commenced auctioneer, to amuse his customers, and Bettison sung with the same view. Mr. B. with his pall, W———y, (then in practice as an attorney) went their rounds, collecting tribute with as much ease as the Dey of Algiers collects his,—and in a similar manner.

About the year 1803, these two Worthies went to work by wholesale, informing against eleven newspapers on the same day, for having inserted advertisements, in which it was proposed to take back a watch which had been lost at Stroud fair, without asking any questions. As this offer was liable to a fine of 50*l.* under what is called Jonathan Wild's act, they had a good pull. However, the whole of the parties stood so firmly, that very little good came of it; on the contrary, one of them took the attempt so ill, that he contrived to *upset their apple cart,* *when afterwards they laid a *fill-*

---

* " Upset his apple-cart," said of one whose whole pecuniary concern is ruined.

away† information against a coal merchant in
Durham yard : they were almost ruined upon that
occasion.   For some years Mr. B. went by the
name of Brown (and Colonel Brown) of Leicester
square ; old B******d, of Gresse Street, being his
nominal informer ; that is to say, he whose name
was inserted in the writ " *Quæré clausum fre-
git*," their favourite mode of proceeding. His companions never mention his real name, or, indeed,
any other, contenting themselves invariably with
the initials only, in the same way we have used it
above.   This did not arise from any dislike to
naming the instrument with which house-maids
excite the fire to burn, but merely to throw
dust into the eyes of by-standers, and to avoid
the painful recollections of Blandford, and of his
lordship's emphatical conclusion, " henceforth
let the name of B——s be infamous, for its present possessor has rendered it so."

Some real lawyers sit about at low public
houses, (and as high ones as they can attain to)
in order to obtain customers, fomenting differ-
ences, and setting friends by the ears.

. We know a score or more of them, whose

▾ † " Fillaway;" to fill the sacks without first measuring
the coals, according to the act.

chiefest practice is picked up in shabby actions arising at public houses, and in markets, as Whitechapel, Leadenhall, Covent Garden and Newgate. So barefaced are they in this nefarious pursuit, that one of them at the last named market, hearing of the editor's intention in collecting materials for the present publication,— offered an indemnity under his hand, if his name and address could be *inserted here at full length.* As this, however, would but give publicity to his paltry mode of practice, we decline to pander to his notoriety: our duty to the public is paramount to every other consideration; and Lawyer —— may have back his intended present by calling at the bar of the same house, where it has lain several weeks, and shall remain to eternity for aught we care for it or him. Had it suited our purpose, we should much rather have inserted a song concerning him which we saw at Pardy's last summer.

OBTAINING MONEY OF SERVANTS,

Under the guise of either bringing some article that has been ordered by the master, or with the false statement that they are sent by him for money or other matters of trade. At times they

have a box or parcel to deliver from the ——
stage coach or mail; the favourite being a basket of *game*, part of which is visible at one
corner, such as the *foot* of a hare, or the *neck* of
wild fowl.   Upon laying open the cheatery, you
have no other present than that I have just mentioned, besides a good hard stone or two, and a
little hay, with which you may wipe down the
perspiration which must hereupon necessarily
supervene.

In all expositions such as these, there is nothing like adducing instances, or as we stiffly
call them " cases;", which have been decided;
and although our *word* is not to be doubted, so
far as we know, the *names* have been as constantly
inserted as they appeared necessary, together with
the *dates*, when they were known or appeared
requisite.

Sir John Sylvester, our Recorder, himself underwent the master-*do* some two or three years
ago, in manner following.   Going to the Sessions
House in the Old Bailey one morning, upon the
grand patter, in much haste, he left his watch
behind; and, vexed at the circumstance, he
opened to Mr. Common Sergeant, " tut! tut!
if I have not left my watch hanging against the
head of the bed !"

A fellow overhearing this, who with a great number of others, was standing upon the steps (all being upon the *kedge*) runs off to Chancery lane with a made-up message, that he was come for the Recorder's watch, which would be found hanging up at head of the bed, and by this token he asked to be believed. What could be more convincing? There the watch hung; and it was delivered accordingly—but never reached the hands of its owner again.

Another plan is, to follow a master or mistress to the butcher's shop, and when they have bought and sent home their meat, to run into the shop with a plate or small basket, for some additional article, stating that the leg of mutton or ribs of beef (as the case may be) which was sent in just now, are not to be dressed to day. This scheme will do for any open shop trade, where the customers can be seen from the outide; and the only precaution against it is, for trades-people so exposed not to *deliver* their goods to the applicant, but to *send* them home.

It is not always, however, people can be aware of this imposture. A young woman, with a child in her arms, knocked at the door of, and enquired for, Mr. B————. He was not at home, she

knew before hand ; so she stated, that he had
been at Mrs. Salmon's wax work exhibition, and
ordered some little pricked pictures which lie
there for sale, upon which he had left two shillings ; the remainder of the purchase, eight
shillings and sixpence, was to be paid to the
bearer, she said, and became very importunate
for the money. However, his maid servant was
sufficiently awake to thwart her imposition concerning the pictures, as well as an attempt she
made to leave the child and run off! but the
butcher's man came into the kitchen with a tray
of meat while she sat there, and she left the house
soon after : going to the butcher's shop, she chose
a piece of beef, which she *took home*, the man an-
swering for its "being all right," as he had
just seen her at the house. The child not having
been employed upon the latter part of the transaction, induces a belief that she had a companion.

Jonathan Harris, formerly respectable as a
ribbon dresser, in Foster lane, was examined at
Guildhall, in August, 1817, on charges of having
delivered baskets and other packages, purporting
to have come by coaches, for which he demanded
the carriage and porterage charges, at various

sums. He was committed specifically for thus taking in a bookseller in Paternoster row; but was let off at the sessions following, through a mistaken act of lenity.

Women, and costermongers, who hawk about poultry, apples, butter, meat, &c. when they find trade rather slack, will at times make a finish of their day's work by pretending they have been ordered to call with their wares. Such as these seldom impose as to prices; but generally put off aged poultry, or meat that died by the hand of its maker. Plated butter—(i. e. fresh on the outside, tallow in the middle) and such other impositions as may suggest themselves to their ingenuity. Most costermongers are thieves, smashers, and the like. We might have said *all of them;* but choose to leave a hole for some one to creep out at.

Hay and straw salesmen are done out of a load or two occasionally, by a clumsy fellow, whom it is a disgrace not to have detected for a villain at his very first appearance, in this manner. He orders the hay to be sent to a respectable name, at a respectable mews, or a livery stable; where the driver is of course to be paid *on delivery,* but he retires into a neighbouring house to get the money, while the men unload, but never appears again.

REGISTER OFFICES*

For servants, increase in number as they decrease in respectability. The very sight of some of them carry conviction to the coarser senses of the object they have in view: viz. the pilfering of the unwary. Can any servant be so besotted as to suppose, that a master or mistress would enter the nasty holes at which they pretend to supply them with *situations?* Boards are put up with " situations" marked on them, and " wanted," followed by the vague notice of " maid of all work, *in a small family;*" " As footman, *where a boy is kept,*" and other such *addenda,* to make the matter palatable by the idea of little to do,—to gull the idle, and to *draw* the simple of a few shillings.

In walking from Smithfield in a straight line to Finsbury Square, you will find three offices of

---

* The earliest establishment of this nature appears to have been situated opposite Cecil Street, Strand, about the year 1740, and called the *Universal* Register, partaking much of the nature of our modern " Echo Office," embracing every object of useful intelligence.

this description, all on the same side of the way;
and these may serve as a sampler of a great proportion of all the rest.

Money is paid at most of them upon entering
the name, but very few of the pilfered servants
obtain what they seek,—a good place; most of
them go without any, or are referred over to
such as it would be beneath them to accept of.
This is done to amuse them; and the poor
deluded creatures exhaust their little stocks
in subsistence, and are driven on the town;
whilst the shark, who pockets the deposit money,
and laughs in his sleeve, sends them to houses
which never thought of employing him, nor of
discharging their present servants.

But there is reason to believe worse, practices
than these prevail at some of them: of one we can
speak with certainty, that not long ago the same
house was a b——y house, and a receptacle for
female servants out of place, as well as a Register
office for servants,—most of whom are females.
We often pass the end of *Maiden lane*; and if
upon enquiry we find there is cause to do so, this
passage shall be softened before it goes to press.

Very few register offices for servants occur
within the city of London *proper;* but among

these, the most respectable, and piquing itself upon being on the most "equitable plan," has been open to the shocking depravity of "the son;" who with our eyes have we seen, and with our ears have we heard, in libidinous intercourse with female servants, applying at his father's office;—we forbear saying more at present: four or five years may have worked mighty alterations; but what has happened may happen again, whatever the fatalist may say.

After all, these offices, properly conducted, are greatly convenient to servants as well as employers; therefore it is more especially the duty of moralists to take care they do not devolve into brothels, or worse. No doubt exists, that procuresses or bawds often hire female servants from register offices, for the purposes of their customers. Generally, the seduction goes on slowly; the *victim* of their delusion being engaged by some modest friend or middling tradesman; and, being sent to the bawdy-house with messages, is there entrapped. One of those many old bawds who live in splendour, keeps three bad houses and one modest one. She is lately married to a fellow, who at Deal sustained the nick name of "King of Prussia." Alie Street *to wit.*

LOTTERY OFFICES.—INSURANCES, AND GOES.

Concerning the first of these we must not say an adverse word : there is an act of parliament to make them legal ; and who dares contravene the ordinances of a law so positive, though it sanctions crime, and renders that innocent, which is in itself altogether baleful and injurious ? But we may be permitted to go into figures : we may calculate, that if for every thousand tickets the lottery contains, only ten thousand pounds are divided among the whole, (or ten pounds each,) then every pound paid for a ticket more than ten pounds, is taken out of the pockets of the purchaser ; and is so much lost, thrown away, or cheated out of you. The half ticket would then be worth *five pounds*,—the quarter ticket *two pounds ten shillings*,—the eighth *one pound five shillings*,—and the sixteenth *twelve shillings and sixpence*. On the contrary, at present, the sixteenth is charged *twenty-seven shillings*, and the whole ticket *twenty* pounds ! and what for ?

Answer that ye knaves ! Tell us how it comes to pass, that the capital. prizes are *never drawn* until towards the latter end of the drawing ?

s

All that has been said hitherto about insurances upon lottery numbers, must undergo revision. We might as well talk of carrying Thames water a horse-back to Islington, or of the advantage of hand spinning over the machines, as to describe the methods of obtaining insurances. Their baleful effects on the deluded wretches who were the victims of the practice, or of the circumventing policy of those who by means of pigeons contrived to *do* the insurers. Nearly all the regularly licensed lottery offices used to become insurers : some of them did a great deal, and employed a great many " collectors of numbers ;" of whose activity you might form some judgment, by placing your back against the Mansion-house on the first morning of drawing, and turning *eyes right*, note the buz at the back doors in Lombard Street, when the first drawn ticket is announced. Although very little insurance can now be effected, on account of the new mode in which for several years the lotteries have been drawn, yet that little is attempted; and we heard with surprise that P. D———ns, an amiable good sort of a regular foolish kind of a lottery office keeper, lost nearly all his property, by means of the old clumsy artifice of *two poll one*.

That is, where two persons combine to cheat a third.

, Peter's confidential man and collector regularly brought in his book at the proper minute; but by leaving a vacancy open a page or two back, he was enabled to insert the number of the first drawn ticket with the name of his confederate annexed to it, which number was brought to him, and dropped into the cellar by that confederate, after the doors had been long locked up, according to act of parliament.

. That collector, whom it will be recollected we have not yet named [*David*] *use* to set at work a *little go* for several years just over his *regular office;* but a lady, whose losses were too much for her temper, took in dudgeon the sullen behaviour of the blind goddess who holds a wheel in her hand; so applied at the shrine of the blind " He who holds a sword in one hand and scales in the other:" they put down his table, and the office is extinguished.

At the west end of the town *little goes* are strewed about in great plenty, and in *the season* double their activity as well as their number. They are of various descriptions; the master of the house always taking a profit on the play, for

which he finds refreshments of the most costly
kind. In this providing, the houses vie with
each other in sumptuousness ; wines of all sorts,
and viands of the costliest kinds, are always at
hand. Five *per cent.* [on all the money won,
pays him well for this; which is the profit or
allowance, on such games as Whist, Faro,
Rouge et Noir, &c.   At E. O., the bar E. bar O.
falls to the master for the same purpose. When
rank cheatery begins, tis called *a do.* .

But if these are the *regular* profits of his trade,
what do not they not amount to when he is *game
enough* to provide a table with a false top ? This
is the modern method of fleecing, and the master
is sure to be in it : this is the *sine qua non* of
the *speck ;* for who would be at the expence,
and run the risque of discovery, were he not to
divide the *Cole ?*

GAME PUBLICANS.

Although numerous laws bear down and grind
the publicans, and render the keeping a small or .
low house little better than slavery, there should
not be one the less kept in force against them ;
but on the contrary it has been suggested, that
they should be further *compelled* to aid the police
in the detection of criminals, who take refuge

under their roofs. No greater mischief can exist than a GAME PUBLICAN; none more baleful to the morals of youth who may frequent his house, by the encouragement his. smile gives to the theory, and the sanctuary his walls afford to the practice of thieving. Let a man of experience talk lightly of crime before a young man of acute disposition, and the bulwarks of his morals give way, then is he fit to be enlisted into the first knot of desperate fellows who may sally forth, to make a prey of the defenceless and the unsuspecting.

The major part of those who keep public houses of the second, third, and lower degrees, are men who have filled menial situations in life; of course they are not expected to exhibit much refinement of manners; civility being the nearest approach to it, they ever reach, and that is enough in the general way. It were well if 'twere no worse. Some are churls, and endeavour to controul those they cannot persuade to deal with them; others are unjust, and take advantage of those whom chance throws in their way; others again, *cheat*, by what is called *chalking double*, or charging more liquor than has been taken. Not a few of those combine also the Swindler with the other parts of their character, in learning to beat their

customers at playing the usual games, as skittles
or back-gammon, cards or dominos, by means of
all the tricks and turns to be found in each,
which they most sedulously acquire of pedestrian
professors. Does it not savour strongly of the
Swindler, for a man to sit hours upon the stretch
at the Bagatelle board, to learn of a Sharper how
to accomplish any given number ? So that the
next customer that comes in to play with him is
quite certain of losing, whatever the stakes may
be ?

But crying as are those evils for redress, they
vanish into smoke before the superior magnitude
of permitting public houses to be kept by men
who have been *had up* for imputed crimes ! Returned lags, though they are the best defined
villains, are not more dangerous than those whose
doings are known to subject them to the laws.
They dare not object to any thing that may be
proposed ; witness he in High Holborn, who permitted the cart-load of hosiery to be unlade at
his house of a Sunday morning, which had that
night been stolen from a shop ? and all this
against his better judgment; for the adage is not
a good one, which says "the more public the
more private." Again, I know that Georgey
C——n, in Tottenham Court Road, was desirous

of *leaving off* several years, but could not (least-
wise he told me so) ; but what was my surprise,
after years of absence, (notwithstanding George
died in the mean time) to find the house in the
same line. Coming out of Bedford Square, eyes
right ! there I saw ten or twelve of the oldest
hands on town, sunning themselves at the door !
The new man I found had been one of those concerned in the affair respecting the buying of
hay in Whitechapel, at Hill's public house, and
is supposed to have *sacked* all the money.

Cripplegate is supposed to be that Ward in the
city, the police of which is the best regulated of
any, and most carefully watched ; but I know
two *game publicans* in it, whose houses are well-
known haunts for night robbers—more or less.
Standing with your back at the church-door, and
stretching out your hands, not quite straight, you
shall find one of them at fifty yards to the right ;
the other stands about two hundred and fifty yards
to the left hand, having a small sinus or elbow still
farther to the left. It is a strange coincidence
that upon going into either of those four houses
you *step down* (more or less) out of the street ;—
the last mentioned having *two* good steps ;—
with the two first the descent is but just per-
ceptible.

Will it not seem strange, that a public house should be a receptacle for rogues, two and twenty years, and its licence still continue; and this, although John Greatorex, at the other end of *the road*, lost his licence without cause assigned? The magistrate who said "that he granted a licence to a house which had been put down for a year, *because* he did not like to hurt the property; and because the house had been newly fitted up in a *tasteful manner;*" adding, that "the *walls* had committed no crime!"* gave but a puerile excuse for one of his numerous partialities. I never go down Bethnal green without thinking of him, and his associates, with a grin.

THE PUBLIC BREWERS AND DISTILLERS

Are deserving of notice here, from the quantity of manœuvring they are always at with their customers, with the public, and with each other. Their conduct towards the publicans is of the most unjustifiable nature (we hope there are exceptions) : these are accused of not filling their measures, which they attribute to the quantity of air that the machine forces into the beer; but one

---

* See Police Report of Examinations before the House of Commons' committee.

or two, more ingenious than the rest, confess they are driven to adopt the fraudulent practice, because they do not themselves receive measure from the brewers.' A late writer* has exposed this matter fully, (and much praise is due to him for the exposition) by giving the particular modes in which the butts are so rendered deficient in their contents, which ought to be one hundred and eight gallons each, whereof two are expected to be ullage, or bottom. But Welby King says, he has measured butts out of which only ninety-nine gallons of proper porter could be drawn; and we understand, that through his representations, many cask-alterations have taken place,—though not to the full extent of the complaint.

What can the poor publican do? Should he complain, he loses his licence, if the brewer has the ear of the magistrates, as we have seen proved.† That is, if he holds a *free* house, and the brewer holds the lease, and with it the customary " warrant of attorney," Messrs. Brewer and Co. enter

---

* In the New Monthly Magazine for 1 January, 1818.

† *Vide* Police Report of the House of Commons; which ought to be read by every body, and studied by all concerned in public house licences.

up judgment, "*Fi fa*" his goods and chattels,
and put in another man who will *take it* more
kindly; one who more obsequiously draws their
rot-gut stuff, and recommends his customers to
cure themselves on the spot with *cordial* gin.

N. B. One scarcely ever gets a drop of good
beer at a mere gin shop; these appear to me to
choose the brewer who sells the worst article.

Bad goods disgust the public, and that with
short measure, hastens the ruin of the suffering
publican; hence the great number of *moves*
(removals) that happen daily, to the great surprise
of every one who does not trace effects up to their
sources; and to the advantage chiefly of the
brokers of spirits, and the appraisers of goods—
who alone reap the harvest that is produced by
bad beer. Moreover, that brewing concern, however rich, is sure to go to wreck, sooner or later,
which serves the public with a bad article, be-
haves harshly to its retailers, or disingenuously
to their fellow brewers. We know them. This
latter description of conduct is the least interesting to the public; for, who cares when two tigers
tear each other's hides? But we cannot help
thinking, that the brewer, who *carneys* with,
fawns to, or, by hook or by crook pays a magistrate, to act unfairly towards another brewer, will

do any dirty work. The employer and employed being equally bad.

The distillers play an under-game generally, unless where a gin shop has a great trade, and then they are the chief creditors. For more on this subject see under the head "smuggling," "private distillery."

SYCOPHANTS,

Or *useful* men, as they are called, abound now more than ever, in consequence of the recently depressed state of our manufactures. They arose out of the latter description of people *on the town*; for, as a bad trade produced Jobbers and Mock-auctions, with the Duffers and the Barkers, so the whole combined gave life to a race of men hitherto undefined, who ought to be termed "Sycophants," because they are so. These, notwithstanding they seem to have much knowledge of the world, owe their depressed situation in life to the very want of that knowledge being carried into practice; and yet it is by the tender of their services in the way of information and advice, that they prey upon the unsuspecting part of the community. Whatever is to be done, they tender their advice, and offer their assistance, asking in return to fill a glass out of your bowl, or to partake of your dish; at least, if they do not put the question, their gentle hints it is impossible to mistake.

Of all qualities and all pretensions, they are to be found at every public house, tavern, and dining-house; where, if you tell ever so inane a story, they are the first to commend, and they laugh at what is *meant* for a joke, although it should be egregious nonsense. Make a display of your purse, and these fellows will lick the dust from your feet; though you mistake so palpable a matter as the hour of the day, they are ready to swear you are right; their politeness is fulsome, their panegyrics nauseate. Sam. Ireland's definition of them was a good one: he termed them "toad-eaters," who would swallow any one's poison.

Are you in doubt what road to take, or how to fashion your taste for *vertu?* The sycophant can direct you better, according to his own shewing, than any one alive. They are to be found plying at the *hotel,* as well as the *watering-house;* and although I am not admitted at either the Blenheim or Long's, yet I have seen them at places standing equally high with those fashionable houses. I have met with them at the Old Bailey Eating houses, at the Chick-lane soup

houses, and in every gradation thence upwards;
but, they are my readers of the middling classes,
who are the likeliest to be exposed to their malig-
nant influence, when they enter the houses of refreshment adapted to their respective circumstances.   Unless they mean to be willing dupes,
let them reject the proffered civilities of such
geqtry : the rough-hewn contradictions of the
blunt countryman, or the man of strong mental
powers, are to be prized ten-fold before them.

And yet, though these sycophants may be despised for their servility, they are not to be reproba-
ted too deeply : they have *bought* a knowledge of
the world, and they would sell it again, and those
who have a wish to become purchasers are merely
cautioned not to pay too dearly for what they
receive.   Undoubtedly, much town-talk information from men *retired* from trade, is very desirable, always entertaining, and sometimes profitable; yet the chances are so much against the
latter, that 'tis two to one the stranger gets done
out of his property—more or less. The thorough-
bred sycophant may be known by his *carney* or
small talk, or by his whining; by his mouth being
always open, either to communicate something,
or to partake of your refreshments.

Generally, they have little second rate trades-

men at hand, whom they recommend you to make
purchases of; these put their heads together, the
one to impress you with a good idea of the goods
and the vender, and the latter to put on extra
profits, the better to divide with the sycophant,
a decent sum at your expense.   Another set are
actually in trade at the moment, if that can be
called *a trade,* which consists of a shop of *all
sorts ;* these are called " general dealers," and
partake much of the character of the jobbers;
only that the latter for a shop, keep a " warehouse," upstairs in a garret; or their lodging
room at the public house serves the purpose of
a *warehouse !*   I have known one of these, at the
same time a dealer in cutlery, coffins, pictures,
paper, hose, books, bandanas, and other heterogeneous articles; while he could recommend you
" to the best brandy merchant in town,"—" a capital good woollen-draper"—" the man that
makes the best boots you ever wore"—and " the
tightest *fit* for a pair of breeches, ever heard of."
With the whole of these, he has " dealt largely
for years ; and all his friends who have bought
of them were perfectly satisfied."

Such is the exact portraiture of a man whom
we have particularly noticed ; and we know as
certainly that the same *genus* of traders abound,

who, though they are far from criminal, ought to
be avoided, as indeed should the whole class of
sycophants from top to bottom. These fellows,
or rather another species of them, have been, not
unaptly termed

SPONGERS, ·

Because they lick, or suck up, whatsoever they
may touch. They are bolder, and more forward
than the preceding, who are thus termed : they
are a lower-bred set; will accost you in the
street with a proffer of their services; the same
in a watch house (if you get into a row), they
can show you to a lodging, where previous to
going to bed, a supper is ordered, and you must
pay the shot. They also differ from the former
class, inasmuch as they can perform none but
puerile services, such as administer to your sensual appetites ; and unblushingly partake, without
even the pretence of bearing a part of the expense. For the most part they can sing a good
song, which they set a going; or tell a hundred
good stories to increase the jollification. If you
would have a *bit of spree*, they can help you into
it; but in helping you out again, they manage
to keep something for themselves out of the necessary fees to the watchmen and constables,

with whom the sponge is the chief negociator
next morning.

Should you ask for a song, appoint a meeting,
or applaud any thing he has said or done, the
Sponge will turn round sharply and ask for the
loan of a few shillings. He will pimp for you,
while talking of his independence ; he will brush
your coat, or carry your umbrella, while boasting
of his connections, and exult that " he enjoys a
moderate competency, in which he feels more
real happiness, than with the comparative splendour of former days, accompanied by the shackles
of his relations' narrow prejudices." Lest this
should not give you sufficient confidence in his
exalted origin, he pulls off his hat to the car-
riages of nobility and gentry as they pass along,
of the owners of which he knows no more than
you do.

One of these gentry walking up the Haymarket
with his new-found companion, was carrying the
umbrella of the latter as well as his own, whilst
the countryman was buttoning his great coat, the
better to resist a threatening storm : Our Sponge
called out, as a carriage drove past, " I'll die if
I shall not hear of this again! Lady T—— will
wonder what I am a doing with two umbrellas
at once. But I shall give her as good as she

brings; the truth, indeed, the truth will serve
my turn best: I shall tell her that I was accompanying a friend from the country, whom I esteemed, (which is truth) to see the Panorama, and the
Museum, and so on. She cannot fail to recollect
seeing you walking at my side; yes, yes, she will
recollect the colour of your coat; Aye, aye, yes,
yes; Oh, she, Sir! She is a good,—as good a
creature! God bless you! Lady T—— against
the world,—if I had money."

The countryman stared at the carriage pointed
out, as it turned round in the street to take up
its fare a few doors above where they stood: a
nursery maid and child were in it; the mother
of the child, perhaps, and mistress of the carriage, having alighted to make some purchases at
the druggist's shop. This was a complete explosion of the Sponger's pretensions, and his character stood fully exposed.

SWINDLERS.

Their arts and boldness assume so many Protean
features, that we despair of giving the reader any
thing like so complete an idea of their practices as
we have of some (if not most) other modes of
taking money out of the pockets of the honester
parts of the community. Our chief difficulty

lies in not being able to give our proofs, or instances, of their evil deeds, with the names attached to them ; for these two reasons, among a
multitude of others : 1. That the endeavours of
honest men, to extricate themselves from difficulties into which they have unavoidably fallen,
partake so much of the arts and practices of the
swindlers to get into them, that we might by
possibility confound one of the former with a
hundred of the latter,—a thing by no means congenial to our feelings ! 2. That those rogues–in-
grain not unfrequently experience such reverses
of fortune, that they face about in the world,
look up, and bring actions to recover damages for
defamation against their *detractors.* We seek
none of these.

To *swindle,*—to take away by undue means,
not to be called robbery, but which is, in effect,
robbery, is the definition of the term which designates the men we are going to treat of.

They are known, in the various situations into
which they are thrown, from the honest fair trader,
by the presumption of their views, as regards
trade in particular; to which they are almost
(but not quite) exclusively attached; but in fact,
to whatever they pretend, it is in a fever ;—in
manner boisterous, forward, petulant, and assum-

ing. In short, all that is disagreeable to the se-
date, discriminating, part of the commercial
world, is to be found in the swindler. He not
only talks higher, but dresses higher; his pretensions to the commonest intelligence, upon the
commonest topics, is always overcharged, and disgusting to moderate men. He has a warehouse,
—or a counting house; perhaps *chambers* in the
city — (those doubtful progeny of declining trade)!
" How are they furnished ? or how filled ? Whereabout does he live, or lodge, or lie ?" Answer
1. Empty shelves; few books, but none of magnitude or long'standing ; and as for the *chambers*, what are the other occupiers on the same
spot ; and how long have they been in their present state, or ·*he* an occupier of them ? To the
second I answer, that he *lives* upon his wits,
lodges any where, and *lies* every where.

How nearly do these approximate to the other
cheats we have described ! viz. Smugglers,
Duffers, Mock auctioneers ? Only differing in
this, that these latter are *sellers*, for money; the
Swindler is a *buyer* of goods without money, (for
which he substitutes " his own bills :") the one
sells in *detail*, at a *careful* price, the other *buys* at
any price; credit being all he looks for.

Swindlers generally take a shop, counting

house, or warehouse, the door of which is always
fastened. When you enter it, a certain degree
of consternation sits upon the countenance of the
person placed there to take in messages. ·The
master is never in the way ; most frequently at a
neighbouring tavern or public house ; or the attendant directs you to Change, where you may
perhaps find him outside the *door* of Tom's or
Batson's,—unless he has a bill overdue, and then
he is at a porter house, in a corner, taking a
sneaking chop by himself. And yet, after you
have come at all those particulars, and drawn
your conclusions ; having made up your mind,
and told him your reasons for discredit, he will
fly at the imputation put upon his character, (for
it is *tender*) talk of his bills in the market, and
other overcharged stuff ; and ultimately succeeds
in hermetically sealing your mouth with the
threat of an action. And the more certainly
would he have recourse to law, as he was more
sure of the imputation being just. This is the
case even with houses of honour and probity,
when under difficulties, but not otherwise. Fear
exists in proportion to the degree of danger apprehended : if there be no danger impressed upon
the mind, no fear can exist in the heart.

  We will adduce two cases in point, of mercan-

tile houses, as honourable and as upright as ever
were unfortunate. We should name them with
regret were it not that the feeling of our duty is
paramount to our ideas of delicacy; when men
choose to make their concerns the subject of a
newspaper squabble, or of argumentation in a
court of law, they must not complain at being
quoted in the evanescent publication now under .
hand. Their cases, and their names, must pass
away with the occasion that gave them birth, to
make room for other newer and better recognised
instances of the overweening care usually bestowed upon that which is of small value : Nurses
usually take the most care of sickly children.

From five to nine years ago was a time of trial
for the strongest mercantile houses in this country.
The successes of the enemy, the burning decrees,
the shutting up of one continent, and the war-
like attitude of another, with its *lucky hits* at sea,
promised fair to ruin the best prospects of the
most firmly established merchants here, who looked to those points for the return of their capital,
with its attendant profits.

Under these circumstances, we heard without
surprise of the stoppages that were daily announced or hourly predicted; but we certainly

saw with grief, in the Times newspaper a dispute
between a Mr. H———re of Bishopsgate and
Mr. S———s, of the house of P. and S., as to
some expressions used by the former respecting
the stability of the latter. The slander was re-
butted, and the utterer swallowed his words.
But the house stopped soon after !

At Guildhall, an action for words spoken, so as
to hurt the character of Messrs. W———d and
Co., was brought against Mr. ————, and a verdict obtained with commensurate damages.
These were scarcely paid, however, when that
house offered a composition and paid it.

We repeat it, these instances are adduced in
order to illustrate our subject, in the same manner as diamonds are best seen in the dark, which
they almost render visible, or at least make us
know its existence.

No man feels the want of character so much as
the Swindler; or laments its absence in his speculations when foiled, or is more waspish in
defence of its latent particles, as they fly off in
the prosecution of his negotiations. The man of
sterling credit, on the contrary, upon finding the
least let or hindrance to the completion of a bar-
gain, relinquishes the purchase with silent indig-

nation, and says (or thinks) "you may keep it
yourself" for aught he cares about you. The
Swindler on the other hand defends himself, and
his credit (creditableness) most pertinacoiusly ;
demands the grounds of refusal ; offers more
references as to character, and shows the cloven
foot of his calling, by insolent insinuations against
the vender.

This sort of reference for character is their
favourite mode of bolstering up each other. It
frequently happens, however, that the party referred to is not a whit better known, or of longer
standing, than the referror ; at times they open
two or three such counting houses on purpose to
carry on the farce of reference. But he must be
a dolt indeed who is duped by ever so many such
references, where the aspect of (no) business is so
much akin to each other. The upshot of such
undertakings is either the King's Bench, the
London Gazette, or a voyage to America ; the
latter being of rarest occurrence, as it always is
for *deep game*, or large consignments to that
quarter ; and the former of daily recurrence,
being for numerous smaller debts, or in case
wherein the effects are so completely swept away,
that scarcely enough remains to pay for working

the commission : Such "*take the benefit*,"* as it is too briefly called.

Goods obtained in the manner we have before alluded to, and paid for in their "own acceptances," they sell for cash, at thirty, forty, or fifty per cent. loss, to auctioneers, to Jews, and the receivers of stolen goods, unless when they are shipped off to America. there to wait the Swindler's coming, among congenial minds to dwell.

However strange it may seem to our readers, there live in great apparent respectability, not to say splendour, many men who deal largely in stolen goods ; and we could walk all the way from London Bridge to Limehouse-hole without once losing sight of some one or other great man's house, who, before the formation of the Docks, was not a great rogue in that way,—knowingly guilty. People may be found in every rank and station, who do not resist the temptation of buying cheap, without reflecting how the goods were come by ; or if the reflection does arise, they stifle it at the birth in the abundance of their cupidity. Wholesale dealers, too, of high and untouchable character, there are, who do

---

* ——" of the Act for the relief of Insolvent debtors," should be understood ; but cramp words and half sentences are generally used to soften down crime.

not blush to make purchases at such prices and
amounts as can not leave a doubt for what end
the goods were obtained. We know of one house
in the linen trade, with whom this culpable practice is so palpable, that their conduct has undergone investigation in a court of law. In the same
street (one of the *newest built in London*) is a
hosier of the same stamp ; with whom, if a manufacturer at Nottingham or Derby is known to do
business, the poor wretch loses his credit for wool
and for cotton and every needful *et cetera.*

When one of those is *upon the go,* that is to say,
must shortly decamp, his acceptances become at
any body's command ; and it not unfrequently
happens, that a shabby fellow has more of these
moon-shine bills proved under the commission
against him, than he could possibly have the address to put forth in five years " for value received." Twenty *per cent* is sometimes paid for such
pseudo acceptances, which are often given before
the bill is drawn (upon blank stamps)—but ten
per cent. or less contents them ; and it happens
frequently that the poor devil only gets laughed
at for his pains before the ink is dry. An honest
man's acceptances, who having stood for years,
yet, who is " upon the go," are sought after with
avidity, at twenty *per cent.* paid down. He is to

U

be pitied who get into such trammels; but falling into one difficulty, draws him on to another;
and the endeavour to extricate himself by one
factitious acceptance but brings on a second and
a third. The forced endeavours to negociate
these, bring his condition to the knowledge of
the Swindlers; who, taking advantage of his situation, demand peremptorily, under pain of dis-
closure—other and more copious sacrifices of his
real creditors' property; and the disgraceful
alliance (as it is considered) attaches to his character through life. When he has gone through
the Alembic of the Gazette, or the Insolvent
Debtor's Court, he is not (as he ought to be)
estimated among the *honest but unfortunate*
victims of *the times,* in which we live, but is
driven by the universal ill opinion of his former
friends, companions, and associates, to join the
deprecated set among whom mere accident had
thrown him, in the hour of his distress. All our
readers must know how little commiseration falls
to the lot of the poor insolvent, against whom no
imputation can by possibility be raised, [the hand
that holds this pen hath signed to the fact] how
then can *he* expect to come back into society,
against whom malignity can thus point her
finger? He is driven out, to add one more to

the miscreant number, and to perform his part
in the ruin and seduction of others, and to per-
petuate a disreputable set, who prey upon the
commercial distresses of the country, and take
advantage of the ill-disguised necessity there is
for the distressed manufacturers making sale of
their goods to any bidders.

· Some swindlers set up their banks in town and
country, issuing their notes payable to bearer on
demand and otherwise. One of them, very
celebrated for advertising "money advanced on
annuities," and for his debaucheries, kept a
―――― *bank* (so written over his door) for twenty
years at Hyde Park wall, at the sight of which
any reasonable persons might burst their sides
with laughter; but within the low walls whereof,
many unthinking persons have been duped of
their property. But that bank, *without capital*, which promised fairest in modern times, was
that of Hartsinck, and Co., the corner of Birchin
Lane, Cornhill, called the "security bank." Next
in high sounding firm was the Piccadilly bank,
Sir John William Thomas Lathrop Murray, Bart.
and Co. who is now on his journey across "*the
herring pond*" for no good. If that be not enough
for the reader, let him be told that Jew King was
concerned in the transaction.

These attempts were made fifteen and twenty years ago, respectively; but were surpassed in conduct, ingenuity, judgment, and *do*, by one which was opened at Ipswich half that time since; as the whole are *in burlesque* by that which was set up at Hammersmith, that drew upon its founder—a coal-shed man in Fleet Lane!

We forbear to put names to these latter ridiculous, but not unsuccessful attempts; but the Ipswich peoples' *fracas* about their character;—the regularity with which their notes were paid for a time by the agent, or accomplice, in Change Alley,—his theatrical demeanour, and shew of business, which went even to the fittings up—show altogether that this was not the plan of a half witted fellow.

Bankers issue their own notes with the most laboured assiduity, and much expence, in order to make a show of business at their correspondent's in town, or to obtain an evanescent character for their names. A Welch banker, one Fr——s F——e kept a traveller at vast expense to journey from London to the Land's-End, solely to disseminate his *cash* notes for bills on London. Vide John S*m*rs.

At times the industrious efforts of Swindlers

devolve into blacker crimes, for which they undergo charges of various hue, from petty larceny up to *capital*.

Not many years ago, a gang of miscreants, who rented a house in Hatton Garden, for the purpose of reference, and were connected with one or two other establishments of the same nature in the city, were found to have locked a man in the cellar, and decamped. When the cries of the poor fellow brought assistance, he turned out to be a banker's clerk, who calling with a bill for payment, they seized and bound him, taking away all the money and assets which he had in charge. They were never discovered.

A clergyman (of the thump craw kidney) who was F. R. S. (i. e. Fellow Remarkably Sharp,) and who was *over fond* of learning, had *a call*. This was not *the call* from above, but one from below, and inappropriately he put it in *experience* upon Parsons of Fleet Street. Here he looked out as many books as filled a bag, with which the boy was to accompany him to a house, he should direct; "it was only in New Bridge Street." When the pair arrived at the door of *an empty house*, our *clergy* knocked at it, and ordered the boy to fetch a certain other book: As nobody answered his application at the empty

u 3

house he bolted with the bag, which became good prize. This was made a criminal charge of, but would not stand good; nor would the lesser one, of "obtaining goods under false pretences;" for he took the precaution of obtaining an account of the books, in which he was made *debtor* for every article; and he afterwards served his *time* out in the Fleet.

ADVERTISEMENTS in the newspapers, of the most captivating kind, are meant to entrap the unwary by their apparently ingenuous offers. At times they offer loans of money, or want to borrow at extravagant interest; oftener they have a trade or well accustomed shop to dispose of, or an invention for which a patent has been obtained;—all these may be known by the eagerness they evince to get hold of the deposit, which is usually demanded; their hurried manner, pompous pretensions, and volubility, declare at once their views. Some years ago, one of them (named a few pages higher up) opened an office for forming matrimonial alliances; a bugbear that soon became exposed by the baseness of its conductor, whose views were directed towards the pockets of his dupes so flagrantly, as to approach the character of crime to that robbery, —only with more finesse.

RECEIVERS

Of stolen goods (or, as they are better called by
their nick name, FENCES and HEDGES) are pretty
well known to the police officers, as well as the
thieves. But as those of them who deal in the
least bulky articles, change their *places of call,*
neither the one nor the other ever *nose the snoozing ken,* where they inhabit. It is the poor de-
vils who are "dealers in marine stores," that are
made obnoxious *by act of parliament.* There is
an adage that says, "the receiver is worse than
the stealer," and so they are, more especially
in these times of refined depravity ; not merely
because "there would be no thieves if there were
no receivers," but for the more proveable reason
that the receivers often incite others to robbery, to
obtain the very articles they stand in need of, or of
which they can make the readiest sale. In proof,
whereof, we adduce the case of Mr. Hunter, silk
manufacturer, of Paternoster row, who having sold
and delivered five pieces of silk, various colours, to
Messrs. ——— and ——— in Wood Street, called
upon their neighbour in the same street, with the
offer of others of the same article ; but what was
his surprise to hear, that they had been offered
goods precisely similar, at prices very little more

than the cost of the raw material? He was still more astonished on calling two or three days afterwards in order to renew the negotiation, to find among the bargains, some three pieces of his own making, part of the identical five above mentioned.

Mr. *Lazarus* of Brick lane, Whitechapel, was the vender of the cheap commodity, and he *bought* them of some of his own tribe, who had robbed the warehouse at which Mr. Hunter sold them. The losers showed good reasons to the receiver why he should pay down the whole amount of the goods stolen. *Lazarus* being happy thus to compromise the felony in lieu of his *character*, which then stood very high in all money transactions and purchases, and will do so to the moment of this publication.

N. B. Never compromise felony with a receiver, or before an officer (the thief himself would be a safer man) ; for a penalty of fifty pounds attaches itself to the mistaken lenity by act of parliament, therefore, dear reader, beware how you fall into it.

Watches, being a ticklish article, are never held by the theives a moment longer than they can help it ; they are therefore sent off to the *Fence* at once, who in this case is generally a watchmaker. He sets at work instantly in *transmogrifying* it,

so as that the owner himself would not recognize
his property again.   There are two or more who
live in and about Spitalfields, and others beyond
the Tower : of the latter I hear from oft-repeated
report ; the former came to my knowledge in
this way.   Coming from *roost* one morning, the
winter before last, I met old acquaintance,
B——e, in Barbican.   " Where going so early ?"
I enquired.   " To Bethnal Green," was the reply.   I wanted very much to know whereabout
there ; but he was extremely costive of commu-
cation, which only served to raise my curiosity
still higher.   He went off at his usual pace : I
could not follow *personally* [it would look so
——ish] ; so I sent my eyes after him, counting
the steps he took : they were thirty-eight *per*
minute by my watch ; and I resolved to wait until he came back, which I knew must be by that
route, as it turned out, being the nearest way to
Drury lane.   Multiplying the minutes of his
absence by thirty-eight, allowing two minutes for
taking a glass of gin, and two more to speak to
the Fence.   I found it brought me so far as
Fashion Street on the right, and on the left
it might extend to Bacon Street ; for I afterwards paced the same number of steps on the

ground, and found he had taken a *whet* (of gin)
in Spitalfields market.

What was the precise nature of his business
remained to be solved. I went to Covent Garden, and upon enquiry found that two watches
had passed through the hands of a neighbouring
———— housekeeper, where I knew he was *sweet*,
not to say *nutty*, upon the *covess*.   But I learnt
no more for nearly a month, when I met him
again in the same *line* of march : we took our
drops together at the first *vaults* we came to.
Here I suddenly demanded of him " What is
o'clock ?" He would have evaded the question,
but I taxed him with having a watch, for that
" I heard it beating."   This, although a lie,
puzzled his *canister*, and he pulled it forth like
a *gaby*, acknowledged that he was " taking it to
the *Transmuter*," and I sucked him of two dol-
lars for quietness sake.

Of other little offences, we have seen a good
deal that was written formerly, and reprinted
latterly, about Kidnappers and Crimps, of
Pimps, Procuresses, and Waggon-hunters, Baw-
dy Houses, and Conjurors, which, if ever they did
exist as there set down, exist no longer ; the method of *doing* having greatly altered like most

other things in modern times. We are inclined to think those reveries proceeded from the fertile brain of one Harry Lemoine, well known upon the town twenty years ago, in the lowest walks. Time has rendered the whole book obsolete, shewing things as they were, *probably*—not as they are, *certainly*.

From what we have said, and seen, and know of the Police of this Metropolis, as well as that of a neighbouring nation, we do not hesitate to say, that the whole *arcana* must undergo alteration here, and approximate itself nearer to the foreign one,—as near as is congenial to the difference of character of the two people. More energy, greater unity of action, less confidence in individuals, and a corresponding degree of secrecy, comprise the outline sketch we would endeavour to impress upon those in whom the humane task is confided, of lessening the *quality* of crime, as well the *number* of the guilty. A sober, silent, and steady regulation of the present alarming system, will do more than an act of parliament.

CONSPIRATORS AND INFORMERS.

In times very remote we are told, from pretty good authority, men sacrificed by wholesale the

lives of others to their mad ambition, or the
resentment of injuries,—real or supposed. But
that we should live in times when the persons employed in the detection of crime (for which we
pay them) should perfidiously assist in its perpetration ; and not only so, but that subsequently
thereto they should bring the offending wretches
to an ignominious death, and that too *under the
semblance of justice*,—is really too much for us
to think of, without pain and grief. Moderately
as we wish to bring ourselves to the subject, in
order to view with calmness the atrocious deeds
daily passing under our eyes, a deep indignation, crying for vengeance, swells our bosom,
and almost suffocates the whisperings of delibe-
rative retribution. The ardour of the soul out-
strips the chastened mind, in the pursuit of
criminals, such as those we contemplate, and
asks the cool and enquiring hand of justice to
lay on without delay its unsparing vengeance.

Until very lately we had thought the case of
Jonathan Wild and the officers of 1788, the
only instance in England of employed
men bartering in blood for money. We knew
and often *witnessed* the too much avidity of
officers to convict capitally ; and we have seen
and heard with proper feelings, *pretended corro-*

bations of the chain of facts adduced against murderers, brought up for no other purpose under heaven than to have "a finger in the pye," and to come in for a share of "*the reward*,"— that bane and antidote of great offences. We have witnessed executions of several men, who were convicted "according to the evidence," to be sure; but what *sort* of evidence? Were there any officers *in it?* And if there were, what is the conclusion?

N. B. Whoever has occasion to prosecute a criminal, let him above all things turn a deaf ear to the advice of an officer, as to modelling his evidence;—more especially if the charge amounts to a *capital* one, or is likely to do so by such modelling. The unknowing reader can scarcely imagine what arts and finesse are used in this way: at times the *directions given* what to say, are at once pointed, rude, and cruel.

But it remained to these times for us to contemplate the officers immediately employed in *detection* of offenders, actually suborning others, and *assisting them in the commission* of crime, with no other view on earth, than through conviction to receive the reward, which by statute they are entitled to, who bring *capitals* to justice. Here we maintain, that they are not

x

culprits *themselves* who have been set at work by
others to commit offences, but those only are
so who set them to work. It is no more our
inclination than our business here to discuss the
abstract question of right and wrong ; but, neither
in this or on any other occasion, shall we refrain
from maintaining what we conceive to be right
through fear that we should possibly be wrong.
Therefore, it is, we insist that Kelly and Spicer,
the two boys, ordered for execution for having
passed bad notes, are not guilty, morally (every
one will allow), *nor* say we, *are they guilty
legally.* For the youths would not have committed the crime imputed to them, but for the
persuasions of Finney ; that is very certain.
And Finney again would have been most careful
how he dealt in this sacrifice of human life,—
with which he meant to purchase impunity for
his own forfeit life by the *favour of Tom Limbrick*,—had it not been for the well-known
favour bestowed on Vaughan, Johnson, Brock,
Pelham, and Power,* instead of those halters they

---

* Sir Samuel Sheppard (the Attorney General) avowed
that they " deserved execution of their sentences." Debate
on a motion for a copy of the opinion of the twelve judges,
which the minister acknowledged did not exist.

so richly deserved, and had taken so much pains to obtain! and were disappointed. The cry of the blood of immolated victims was before the judgment seat; but so much of state policy and of feverish management, and overweening care, hath marked the two administrations of Lord Sidmouth, from the time of Despard and the Tinman of Plymouth, to that of the Derby row and William Hone, that we should not wonder the least to see the last four named "hellish scoundrels"* FOR THEY ARE QUALIFIED, advanced to some Post or office in the gift of the state.

Mr. Vaughan received his appointment to office a year ago, as inner turnkey of a yard in Cold Bath fields prison, and the pardon of Brock, Pelham, and Power, and of Ben Johnson and Donnelly, was known six months before their liberation took place. And when did it take place, think you, gentle reader? I will tell you: at a time the most *mal apropos* for a thinking mind to reflect upon, that the darkest, revolting, solicitude could have chosen; namely, the very moment that the warrants for hanging Kelly and Spicer arrived at Newgate, saw also come to hand the order to

---

* Mr. Tierney's words.

x 2

liberate those four villains, who had contributed
by their example,—but more by their impunity,
—to induce that equally graceless villain, Finney, to take away the two boys (17 and 15 respectively) by the same species of villainy as they
had practised.

When the keeper of Newgate opened the six
pieces of paper which contained his directions
respecting the disposal of the six men under his
care, he must have resembled much the drawer
of the state lottery, "just two blanks to a prize;"
only the fortune *he* unfolded was of deeper interest, and replete with more painful sensations
of grief, national shame, disgust and horror, at
every turn up, whether these were the blanks or
prizes of the unseemly envelopes which contained
—*death* to the innocent, or *life* to the guilty.

Let us ask oursⁱ ⁱes a question.—What would
have been the conⁱ ⁱt of Limbrick, if one or more
of the five *hellish scoundrels* had undergone the
sentence of the law ? Would he have kept *in
tow* this new scoundrel Finney ? When the latter
was known to him as a passer of bad notes for
many months, did nothing pass upon the subject ? Yes, most assuredly ; and we might venture
to predict *the words* of the conversation, which

terminated with " I dont want *you ;* shew
me the *others.*" Mark the plural, reader !
Two are better than one at any time. So Spicer
was added to Kelly, and both delivered up as
sacrifices to secure impunity to the greater
rogue. Else why not take *him* along with the
other two ? "*I had reasons for it,*" said Limbrick. These reasons are so apparent, so re-
pugnant to our feelings, and so appalling to
humanity, that we forbear to enlarge further,
than by concentrating the whole essence of his
murderous " reasons" in two words; *viz.*
MORE BLOOD ! ! !

Our readers, who are "strange to the ways of
town," will naturally enough desire to be informed of the precise points upon which those
five *hellish villains* were convicted, and of those
graye " reasons," which obtained for them their
pardon, and accomplished their enlargement.
These it is our duty to give. We shall come, at
the conclusion, to this advice : never engage in
any thing unlawful, though your employer be
never so generous ; fall not into habits of intimacy
with strange or doubtful characters (first ascertain who and what they are)—do not let any one
dodge your heels at night or by day. These

precautions are deemed necessary for the decent and respectable part of the community; for, although the chief part of the wretches who have been entrapped into the commission of crimes, were poor,—yet *we* have *reason* to think, the blood hounds will take other grounds, and seek for higher victims. What, for example, is a decent and respectable man (however innocent) to do, when pounced upon and searched, there is found in his pockets a quantity of forged notes, or false coin? No matter how they came there; whether they were dropped into his pocket in the street, or in the public house (while perhaps he was a little drunk);—or whether the base imitations were concealed in the officer's hand, and pretended (*upon oath*) that they were found in his pockets,—his good character, his innocence, will stand him in no stead; but he must, under the present administration of our criminal code, suffer the law, and the officer pockets the money, which is the price and the *reward* of his villainy!

Two boys were served in this manner on Tower-hill, a few years ago, by one of the five *hellish villains* named above: that they were not hanged was through no omission of his, nor did his soul receive any consolation probably from that circumstance; for immediately after that we find him prosecuting a young man, a banker's clerk, for an abominable offence. The officer was the only evidence, and the clerk was pilloried opposite Princes Street, Mansion-house. We know not whether the clerk is dead or alive; nor whether his condemnation and punishment has undergone the same revision as some others: Bill Soames's for instance; he was convicted on the evidence of Vaughan, and that of a man (gentleman!) never heard of before or since; but the enquiry terminated in the remission of the punishment, which shows how little reliance was to be had upon the latter evidence when deprived of the support of the former's. The sweep boy who picked up the pocket book (an empty one!) knew not who threw it away, and his evidence went to nothing more than the mere fact of picking up.

Every one knows how guilty Soames was of numerous other robberies, but no one would say that he ought to be punished upon a *false* charge, or an *entrapped* crime. If this were proper and right, why not, with the confession of the Attorney General before us, that the five *men* " deserved to be hanged," hang them all at once in the

face of a legal quibble? We every day see men
at large, who ought to have been hanged years
ago; and yet it would answer the end of no honest man to step up to one of them, and clap-
ping a noose round his neck, run him up at the
next lamp post.   But if the same culprit were
taken up and tried and *found guilty of the fact*
that subjected him to be hanged, **what signifies
it,** *the law term* that is bestowed upon his crime?
There is too much disposition to *quibble* in our
lawyers: common sense and common honesty are
oft forgotten in that hateful propensity.

Vaughan was convicted of having, by means
of one Davies, a lame petty officer of the navy,
induced **four** youths to break open the house of
a woman with whom Davies cohabited.   Their
hearts failed them at the door of the premises,
and they left the *tools* behind which Vaughan
had furnished to Davies.   However, the devoted
boys were caught *nearly* in the fact, not quite;
for they had not yet made a breach.   This disappointment was foreseen by the wary Vaughan,
and a ring belonging to Davies's woman was by
him slipped into the pocket of one of the victims; upon which incontrovertible corrobation
of the other parts of the evidence the prisoners

were found guilty, and they would have received sentence of death, but for the explosion of the plot occasioned by Davies's *splitting*.

Ben Johnson's offence was in like manner house-breaking. With aggravated circumstances he induced his victim to rob a friend's house, and betrayed him before hand; ordering the usual watchman, who would have *prevented* the robbery, from interfering. This was the second victim he avers that he had so convicted; and boasting to the surviving relations of the first man that such was the fact, he seemed to glory in the crime he had committed and exulted over the wounds which he thus opened afresh. Just as we are writing these incoherencies, the caitiff, who is the subject of them, struts past our view, and exhibits in his gait the improved manners of an unchained felon. He was assisted by one Donelly, who was convicted of the same offence.

Brock, Pelham, and Power, were more complex in their attempt upon three labourers from the sister island, one of whom could speak none but his native Irish. Going to the Cheapside stand, where on Monday mornings labourers offer themselves by scores, these villains agreed with one Renorden and his two countrymen, for a job of work which should be pointed out to them

This was no other than to prepare round pieces
of metal, resembling shillings, by polishing,
filing, and colouring them; the room in Moor
lane having been previously hired, and the materials prepared by the conspirators. In this
miserable hole, after a few hours labour, the three
innocent men were set upon by persons they had
not before seen, conveyed to prison, and in a very
few days were arraigned for treason in imitating
the coin of the realm, for which the sentence is
to be hung, drawn, and quartered.

Enjoying this horrid sight, so congenial to his
feelings, wishes, and views, was Pelham,—one of
the conspirators who had hired the three
victims in Cheapside,—recognised, as he attended
at the press yard of the Old Bailey, by a
labourer who was present at the hiring; after
a struggle, and a *hunt*, Mr. Pelham was secured,
and the plot, by the exertions of the lord Mayor
(Wood), was laid bare.

All those six fellows were indicted *by the city*,
for being accessory, before the facts, to the crimes
imputed to their respective victims; upon the
clearest evidence imaginable they were found
guilty and received sentence of death ; but after
little more than a year's imprisonment we are struck
aghast upon hearing they are to escape upon a quib-
or less than a quibble.   We are alarmed at the

state of society which is doomed to receive again, in these our days, such a pestilence into its bosom, to contaminate entire masses of its most unprotected members ;—those who look up for help, for advice, and assistance to the higher classes, and the higher powers are thus exposed to the cold-hearted callous-souled creators of crime, the murder-manufacturers of these sad times. We feel national shame, and express in weak terms our individual sorrow.

N. B. Since rewards upon conviction cannot be taken away (in sound policy) as has been proposed, the mode of distributing them must be altered ; and also in the first place the power to dispense justice must be taken out of the hands of the officers altogether. What can be thought of the anxiety of an officer to convict capitally, arriving at that pitch as to employ a counsel, and pay the fees himself to induce a jury to bring in a capital verdict, which might possibly have taken a milder turn? Yet this has happened, frequently where the prosecutor has evinced signs of clemency towards the accused.

The least guilty blood-hounds, are those who permit the escape of prisoners for lighter crimes, in order that they may be induced to commit those of blacker hue,—rewardable by statute ; to say nothing of the *hints*, the *put ups*, th *sneers* at justice, the proposed *good understanding*, the jeering at prosecutors, and a thousand other arts, that smoothen crimes, and render even punishment more palatable. These keep their eyes on a given number of culprits, whose movements and haunts they watch with cat-like assiduity, and whom they *catch* as often as they want spoil.

---

* A very circumstantial and lucid account of the base attempt of a Blood hound upon the life of a gentleman under temporary distress, is given in the twenty-second chapter of the " LIFE OF MR. JEREMY FORESIGHT," lately printed. Although highly entertaining, and strictly elucidatory of our subject, the revolting narrative is too long for insertion here, and we refer the reader to that gentleman's own well written account of his complicated affair, and narrow escape.

THE END.

www.ingramcontent.com/pod-product-compliance
Lightning Source LLC
Chambersburg PA
CBHW020345270326
41926CB00007B/325